NOT-lanta

Georgia. Sports. *Cursed*?

Jeff Lalaian

To Maddie,

Wishing you the best. I hope you enjoy the book!

Jeff

NOT-*lanta*: Georgia. Sports. *Cursed*?

Copyright © 2019 by Jeff Lalaian

Text by Jeff Lalaian

Cover Design © 2019 by Elizabeth Jones

All rights reserved. No part of this book may be reproduced or transmitted in any form or by any means without written permission from the author.

ISBN: 978-0-578-22883-9

To Misty

You have been placed in my life by God, you are my best friend and without you I am incomplete

and

To Ellie, Abbie and Hannah

You are amazing young ladies and you make me so proud. Always look to God first and He will supply your needs

Table of Contents

Preface..i
Acknowledgements...v
Chapter 1   The Curse...1
Chapter 2   The Beginnings..................................12
Chapter 3   No Joy In Mudville............................24
Chapter 4   Prime Time…For A While Anyway......32
Chapter 5   Had We Only Known Then.................37
Chapter 6   At Least We Got One..........................49
Chapter 7   The Turning Point..............................58
Chapter 8   Dark Side Of The Curse.....................68
Chapter 9   The Good, The Bad And The Ugly......79
Chapter 10   What Might Have Been......................88
Chapter 11   Salsa With A Side Of Curse...............96
Chapter 12   Almost…Again...................................105
Chapter 13   Groundhog Day..................................115
Chapter 14   Death, Taxes And The Curse.............123
Chapter 15   Dr J, Threezus And El Gigante..........135
Chapter 16   The Grim Reaper Cometh..................145
Chapter 17   The Backup Plan................................158
Chapter 18   28-3…Need I Say More?...................167
Chapter 19   Sisyphus..184

Preface

NOT-lanta: Georgia. Sports. Cursed? is a look at every major sporting event in the greater Atlanta-Athens, Georgia region over the last forty years through the eyes of a fan. I'd like to think I've been preparing to write this book my entire life. From my earliest of memories I have followed the local sports teams – Atlanta Braves, Falcons and Hawks and the University of Georgia Bulldogs football team. Perhaps, "followed" is too passive a term, as I have kept a comprehensive internal record of every big game moment that has ever taken place in this town.

Unfortunately, for myself and any other fan in my vicinity, we have endured a rather sordid sports history. When looking at the circumstances surrounding every consequential moment and game outcome of the teams I support, there is only one logical conclusion to be made – my sports town is unquestionably cursed. My intention is to convince the reader of this terrible and ever-present truth. The evidence will speak for itself as it is laid out in a sequential and consistently mounting manner.

NOT-lanta follows the rise and fall of each season that represented a defining moment for our area. I hope to the bring to the attention of the population at large the anguish and misery our fan base has suffered through during each of those memorable, yet heart-wrenching seasons. Plenty of cities have had bad losses or unlucky moments, but the preposterous amount of misfortune and dastardly turn of events witnessed by my teams will leave little doubt that some nefarious force has been preventing us from achieving glory. Not only that, I will convince anyone who reads this through, that our Curse is by far the most heinous and sinister in all of sports. By the end, there will be little doubt.

Over the course of forty years, my two brothers and I have witnessed every type of excruciating loss and debilitating defeat one could possibly imagine. The conversation of "Curse" has been a hot topic in our family for years. Every time one of our teams collapses or some inconceivable occurrence ends our season, the discussion is always the same. We don't blame the players anymore, nor the coaches or referees for that matter. No, we lay all culpability at the feet of the Curse - a living, breathing entity that, for some reason, is unrelenting in its efforts to derail our success.

At some point, I created a list of "curse moments" that continued to grow season after season. It was always great fodder during family, friend or church gatherings. My brothers and I have parsed over every play, every call, and every decision that has been made and have run out of other plausible reasons as to why we so often fail to come out on top. Victory is always ripped away at the last minute, even when defeat seemed impossible. Why us? Will it ever end?

Over time, the "list" took on a life of its own. Often, I found myself reliving history for others, providing running commentary and memories of each ridiculous Curse moment. Eventually, the endless banter led me to chronicling all that we have experienced as sports fans and try to come up with some rational explanation for it all. In many regards, writing the book served as a cathartic way to heal wounds created from so many sports battle scars. Most importantly, though, my primary purpose in writing this book is to unmask the Curse itself. Adversaries that are nameless and faceless are much more difficult to overcome.

Therefore, my hope is that by exposing the Curse we can ultimately break its formidable grip on our city and state. If this book can, in any way, help "reverse the Curse", then it has accomplished its intended goal. For some reason, other sports curses have become more well-known and well-documented, but ours had conspicuously never been brought to light. It's time to shed the cloak that has surrounded what every sports fan in my town has known for decades. It's time to lay out the evidence piece by piece in a complete and unbiased way, letting the results speak louder than words. It's time to let the world judge for themselves, once and for all. Is my sports town cursed? You decide.

Acknowledgements

First and foremost, I would like to give thanks to God for His goodness and His blessings. I am also tremendously thankful for my family. My deepest gratitude goes out to my wife Misty for her unwavering support throughout the years, in spite of my mild sports obsession. I want to thank my brothers, Danny and Tim, and their families for their love and assistance throughout this process. Danny, thanks for being such a demanding "editor". Julie, thanks for the proofreading expertise. Alexis, thank you for letting me use Tim for all of his "gifts and talents". I want to thank my church, City on a Hill, for the encouragement and inspiration to write this book. Without Sunday Night Fellowship, none of this would have been possible. Specifically, I would like to send a big shout out to Octo-Mike and "Unbelievable" Randy. Also, major thanks to Liz Jones for her amazing and gracious design talents, to my students for always letting me express myself, and to the many others who helped along the way.

Chapter 1

The Curse

Déjà vu! Is it just me, or have I seen this before? 1992 World Series. Atlanta Braves vs. Toronto Blue Jays. Game Six. Charlie Leibrandt, the crafty, veteran (*old?*) lefthander is on the mound for the Braves in an extra-inning thriller. Dave Winfield, the future Hall of Fame outfielder is up to bat with the game on the line.

Wait a second! Did I say 1992? Surely, we've seen this movie before, and we know how it's going to end. It's sort of like when I saw the film *Titanic*. Even though you know the ship will sink, you nevertheless have this faint hope that the outcome really is in doubt. But, of course, anyone that has been around long enough knows exactly what's about to happen. James Cameron couldn't write this script.

It was just a single year earlier that our beloved Braves manager Bobby Cox had the notion to bring fifth starter Leibrandt out of the bullpen in another World Series Game Six extra-inning thriller to face the future Hall of Fame outfielder Kirby Puckett. Yes, Leibrandt is a lefty with little to no zip left in his arm. And, YES, both Winfield and Puckett are right-handed power hitters who eat that type of pitcher for breakfast.

In the 1991 series against the Twins, we all heard the rationale for having Leibrandt face Puckett. The wily pitcher will mesmerize the hopefully over-aggressive hitter with his tempting, yet off-the-plate changeup. I remember thinking in my still innocent and naïve mind, *"Wow, Bobby Cox sure is smart."* For generations, managers have avoided having pitchers face a batter from the opposing side of the plate in situations like these. But this time, we were going to outsmart them all. Leibrandt was going to strike out Puckett, our Braves would take the lead the next inning and we'd all be dancing in the streets as World Series champs. Not only that, with our young core, we could win maybe 3 or 4 or 5 or more championships. Thank goodness for Bobby Cox. His masterful ways will change the fate of our team (*our city? the world?*) forever.

But then, as you may have heard, the ship sank. We all should have known the ship (*our chances of winning the series?*) would be undone by the iceberg (*Bobby Cox?*), and all passengers along for the ride (*Me? The fans? Braves nation?*) were going to drown. Leibrandt did not strike Puckett out. Instead, the future Hall of Famer did what future Hall of Famers are supposed to do. He hit the game-winning homerun that not only proved to be a harbinger of defeat for the Braves in the forthcoming epic Game Seven, it set a precedent that is still holding sway to this day.

Isn't that precisely why managers for generations would have gone righty against righty? Isn't that why they call it "going by the book"? Not us. Not on this night. Now, if Cox had been bringing in, say, Sandy Koufax or Steve Carlton or Randy Johnson, I would have been all in. But Charlie Leibrandt? Really? I would have even settled for one of our other bullpen lefties, Mike Stanton or Kent Mercker. Instead, we went with what seemed like an 85-year-old Leibrandt, with his 75-mph fastball. Yep. Now that's a recipe for certain success. At least we know one of the best managers in the game will learn from his mistakes. The memories of Leibrandt looking over his shoulder as Puckett etched his name in the history books, will surely never be forgotten. Right? Well, not exactly. As they say, those who cannot learn from history are doomed to repeat it. Clearly, Bobby Cox was not privy to this adage.

Fast-forward 12 months. There we were again. Same situation. Same Game Six. But, unfortunately for anyone rooting for the Braves, same managerial decision. If you can believe it, Bobby Cox brought Charlie Leibrandt into the game to face Winfield with the game hanging in the balance. Does the phrase "fool me once, shame on you" come to mind? Anyone? They say if it ain't broke don't fix it. But what if it's actually broken?

I was only 17 years old, but I was sitting there thinking even I knew better than to have Leibrandt back out there. Visions of Puckett prancing around the bases were still fresh in all our minds. We had just scratched and clawed our way back into the game after tying the score in the bottom of the ninth off Blue Jays all-star closer Tom Henke. My hope restored. My faith renewed. This year, we would win Game 6, then claim victory in our own epic Game Seven thriller. But then, it happened.

There are moments in your life where you feel destiny knocking at the door. This was one of them. But destiny is a tricky thing, isn't it? You recognize it when it appears, excited to feel it, but you pray you are not on the wrong side of it. We may not have realized it at the time, but this type of situation was soon to become part of the Atlanta sports fabric. Cue Bobby Cox. Cue Charlie Leibrandt. And cue the inevitable.

As soon as I saw Leibrandt, I must admit, my heart sank. I have nothing against one Mr. Charlie Leibrandt. In fact, I'm sure he's an amazing individual. He must be. How else do you explain Cox putting him in that situation for a second consecutive year? You can't. Maybe he saved Cox's life when he was choking on a chicken wing. Maybe he had pulled Cox out of burning car just before it exploded. Maybe he rescued one of Cox's children (*maybe he was Cox's child?*). Who knows?

But there we were, again. Maybe this time would be different. Maybe this time Leibrandt would actually dance his change-up off the plate and Winfield would whiff. Maybe this time the plan works, and the Braves championship run begins in earnest. Maybe this time destiny will be on OUR side. But it wasn't.

Winfield doubled down the line, bringing home the winning runs. Half an inning later the game and series (*My hope? My innocence?*) were over. Just as had happened the year before, my team was oh-so-tantalizingly close to a championship, only to come up empty in the end. Now, I know my sports history as well as most. Plenty of teams have come up short of the ultimate prize. In fact, many have come up short in back to back years. But something seemed different, if not unusually cruel about this one. To lose once at the hands of Charlie Leibrandt was bad enough. But twice? Was Leibrandt going to end every World Series for the rest of time? My mind was questioning everything. How could such a theoretically great manager make the same mistake in two consecutive years?

That night I began to learn some valuable lessons about my sports teams. It wasn't about Charlie Leibrandt or anyone else that took part in either of those World Series. I wanted to believe that Cox had done me wrong, but this was bigger than him. They were just pawns in a much larger cosmic game. It didn't matter who Cox brought in to pitch. It didn't matter who they would have been pitching to. Except, it WAS Leibrandt both years and it WAS the same result. There was such a diabolical symmetry to all of it. The names on those Braves teams read like a who's who of baseball icons. But it was Charlie Leibrandt who had the ball in his hand both times with the outcome seemingly still in doubt. This would become a common theme to my entire sports fandom experience. The result was always going to be the same - an agonizing, if not traumatizing loss. Outcomes that were so outlandish, it would have been impossible to have even considered such circumstances. Yet, they somehow have become commonplace, if not predictable. Imagine a sports lineage littered with the most devastating chokes, egregious blown calls, and loathsome bad luck. You might tend to become numb to such things. You don't feel the pain any longer. The callouses that have been earned by so many sinister defeats are almost impenetrable.

     I now live in a world where I almost revel in every new twist of the knife (I mean twist of fate). Every unthinkable coincidence that brings the ultimate demise to another season simply serves as confirmation to what we were all expecting anyway. The magical fairy dust is always sprinkled liberally, but never on us. Every year we say it can't get worse, yet every year it somehow does. There is a seeming endlessness to it all. Almost thirty years later, I have finally resolved it in my own mind. I have finally found a peace between my ever-enduring desire for redemption and my absolute understanding that I will never have it. It was all fated to happen. It will always be fated to happen. A lifetime of empirical evidence is hard to ignore………….my sports town is CURSED!

     Sports curses are an interesting thing. You never know how or why they happen. They just do. Arguably the most well-known curse of them all, The Curse of the Bambino, comes to mind. We all know the story. In 1919, the Boston Red Sox, winners of three of the previous four World Series, trade Babe Ruth to the New York Yankees for a mere $25,000. The Yankees go on to win title after title over the next 80-ish years, while the Red Sox become the poster child for Murphy's Law. Everybody knew it – the Red Sox were cursed. Coming up short in winner-take-all Game 7's was all the rage in Boston. See 1946 or 1967 or 1975 or the infamous 1986. Throw in winner-take-all regular season tiebreakers in 1948 and 1978 against the Cleveland Indians and those aforementioned Yankees just for good measure. That's not even considering the litany of American League playoff losses from 1988 to 2003. Legendary names like Bill Buckner, Bucky Dent, or Aaron Boone will be forever linked to this Curse.

But then something happened. The Curse, the history, the folklore all vanished in the blink of an eye. In 2004, the Red Sox overcame history. They overcame a 3-0 series deficit. They even overcame the Yankees, the evil empire themselves, en route to their first World Series title since trading away Ruth. It was over. The Curse was broken. In fact, the Red Sox have now won FOUR titles over the last 15 years. Indeed, I'd say the Curse is no more.

The Chicago Cubs have also suffered through a somewhat cursed existence. Theirs was known as The Curse of the Billy Goat. Legend has it that goat owner William Slanis was told to leave Cubs' stadium Wrigley Field during the 1945 World Series, because his pet had a not-so-pleasant odor. Upon leaving, he supposedly cursed the team from ever winning again. And, as if on cue, the Cubs upheld their end of the Curse for the next 71 years, never reaching the World Series. They became known as "the Lovable Losers". Despite having reputable talent throughout the years, they could never seem to get over the hump. Their history included black cats running across the field at inopportune moments, blown September division leads, and some guy named Bartman, among other things. An entire generation of Cubs fans came and went without seeing a single World Series game. But then, in 2016, the unthinkable happened. The Cubs won it all. Cubs fans all around the world had shed their identity of "always the bridesmaid, never the bride". This time they were the bride, and they walked down the aisle of championship row with the Curse in their rearview mirror.

Now before we begin feeling too badly for fans in Boston and Chicago, let's consider a few important points. While the Red Sox were wallowing in their woe-is-me history, keep in mind that Boston was a championship magnet for all other sports. The Celtics were the Yankees of the NBA, winning a total of 17 titles. The Boston Bruins were winning hockey's Stanley Cup six times. And, oh yeah, the New England Patriots were, well, the Patriots, winning six Super Bowls. And, of course, now the Red Sox themselves are regular title holders. Yep, I sure hate it for those guys in the northeast.

Also, consider fans in Chicago. Yes, the Cubs gave their supporters little payoff for a full century of passionate loyalty, but don't pity them just yet. While the Cubs were only giving us Harry Caray, the Chicago Bulls were giving us some guy named Michael Jordan. I'm sure you've heard of him – and his six NBA Championships. Perhaps you remember the '85 Bears, Super Bowl champs and arguably the most dominant team in NFL history, to go along with multiple league titles in the pre-Super Bowl era. Not to mention, several Stanley Cup wins for the Chicago Blackhawks. As Justin Timberlake once expressed, "Cry me a river!"

Is a curse really a curse if the agony of defeat is regularly coinciding with the thrill of victory? Or does that fall in the "you win some, you lose some" category? What if all you know is the agony, but rarely the thrill? What if the "we'll get 'em next year" mantra is not just for one of your teams, but for all of them? Some say Cleveland seems to fall into this category. Do they? They definitely have had some close calls. The 1980's Browns come to mind. As do the Indians' World Series losses of 1995, 1997, and 2016. The Cavaliers teased us with Lebron James, before breaking their own "curse" with a historically memorable NBA title in 2016. But, I contend, Cleveland (or any other city, for that matter) has nothing on my teams. Even Cleveland fans can boast two Ohio State Buckeyes Football National Championships in the last twenty years. Oh, and don't forget about the Browns dynasty of the 50's and 60's, winning four league titles in nine championship game appearances. Poor Cleveland? Yeah right!

  Losing is one thing. But what I'm talking about goes well beyond simply "taking the L". We've all heard the phrases "adding insult to injury" and "pouring salt on my wounds". Imagine dredging the oceans of every salt particle in existence and pouring it into every open wound of every fan of every team of an entire sports base. You don't just lose. You lose in the most excruciating, can't-believe-my-eyes, epically unimaginable ways. I don't want to hear about the Red Sox, or the Cubs, or even Cleveland, for that matter. They have no idea what I've been through. They would have wilted long ago under the circumstances that I have faced.

  What's worse is that our Curse doesn't even get close to the national respect it deserves. I know I am speaking for a generation of sports fans around me. Where is our ESPN documentary? I firmly believe that I am witnessing the most wretched, most gut-wrenching sports curse of all time. And I think the evidence backs me up.

Let's do a quick rundown. Largest playoff race collapse after September 5 in baseball history. Largest blown lead in SEC Championship Game history. Largest collapse in NFC Championship Game history. Most consecutive Game One losses in baseball postseason history, to go along with the most consecutive series losses in baseball postseason history. Largest second half collapse in the College Football Playoff Championship Game history. Second largest blown lead in a game in World Series history. Oh yeah, and the largest collapse in Super Bowl history.

Do you know what all of these records have in common? They belong to my teams. How is this NOT common knowledge? How has there not been a movie made about my city, my teams and our Curse? The worst part is those records are just the tip of the iceberg. To relive those moments is not necessarily the most pleasurable experience, but our story must be told.

If you haven't already surmised, I am a diehard fan of Atlanta's professional sports teams. I am also a diehard fan of the University of Georgia football team. I am not alone in my belief that my sports teams are cursed. For those outside of my region, it may be the first time you're hearing of this. The curse of which I speak has no catchy name. Maybe that's why it gets overlooked. Let's face it, names matter.

How many of us have heard of the musical group The Quarrymen? That's right, you haven't. You know why? Because some lads from Liverpool decided to change their name to the Beatles. Could you imagine Ed Sullivan, back in the day, welcoming The Quarrymen to the stage in front of a screaming and crying throng of teenage girls? Not likely. Or have you ever seen a movie starring Tom Mapother IV? Believe it or not, you have. *Top Gun. Jerry*

Maguire. Probably the list goes on and on. The thing is, *Mission Impossible* starring Tom Mapother IV just doesn't have the same ring to it as the actor you may have heard of, Tom Cruise.

When naming a curse, it's no different. It's got to have a name that resonates. It's got to have a name that carries a little swag. The Curse of the Bambino has both. The Curse of the Billy Goat has mythical proportions written all over it. Some have tried to give ours a name. The Curse of Turner Field has been bantered about, on the basis of our run of misfortune since it came into existence. Who says that's when the curse even began anyway? I think the facts will show our curse has been an ongoing theme much longer than the last 25 years.

Some suggest our local teams have been cursed ever since we built a stadium on a Native American burial ground. First of all, you really can't name a curse for a completely uncorroborated story. Is there really any hard evidence of what was under the stadium? Do I have the power to be the final word on this issue? If so, The Curse of Turner Field is out. The Curse of the Burial Ground is also out. In my opinion, this all began well before the Braves, or Hawks, or Falcons, or even the Bulldogs took shape. Actually, I think it all began back in November of 1864. Yes, I said EIGHTEEN sixty-four! That's when William Tecumseh Sherman and his men from the Union army burned the city of Atlanta on their game-changing "march to the sea" during the Civil War, attempting to destroy any vestiges of Southern morale. Perhaps this quote from Sherman says it all:

> *"War is cruelty. There is no use trying to reform it. The crueler it is, the sooner it will be over."*

Replace the word "War" with "Sports" in Sherman's quote and you have a sense of what has transpired in the greater Atlanta-Athens area over the last quarter century. It HAS been cruel, and unrelentingly so. I can assure you there are no more "vestiges" of morale remaining. I propose a name for this curse. A name that embodies the full history of Atlanta heartache and heartbreak. A name that has all of the qualities that a curse of this nature deserves. A name that will help the rest of the sports world finally see the truth. I propose we call this phenomenon……………..The Curse of Tecumseh.

It says it all. Atlanta has been a burning heap of sports misery and disaster for years. Even better, Sherman was named Tecumseh after the Shawnee warrior and chief who sought to unite tribes and form an independent Native American nation. Chief Tecumseh, as it is told, traveled South, attempting to gather as much tribal unity as possible. Unfortunately for Tecumseh's cause, he was rebuffed when he reached Georgia, and his goal of an independent nation was never achieved. Pretty ironic, if I say so, myself. If I may put two and two together, it appears that the state of Georgia and the name Tecumseh have a rather sordid past.

Is this a name we can all get behind? For some reason, having a name for this monstrosity is cathartic. As we've all heard, you can't overcome a problem until you admit you have a problem. I admit it. We have a problem. Perhaps, in my heart of hearts I feel that this acceptance is the first step in actually breaking the Curse. In many ways, I'm still that 17-year old boy at heart. I still have dreams of glory, even if they are delusions of grandeur. But one thing I know for sure, the Curse of Tecumseh is real. If you don't believe me now, you will.

Chapter 2

The Beginnings

I was born in 1975 and raised in the small town of Loganville, Georgia. There was nothing special about the town, other than Eleanor Roosevelt once dedicated a building there in the 1930's. Loganville, however, sat almost perfectly between the cities of Atlanta and Athens. Our little Angus cattle farm was right on Highway 78. Go out of my driveway and you were 40 or so minutes from either city, depending on whichever way you turned. My sports allegiances should be fairly obvious. Atlanta Braves. Atlanta Falcons. Atlanta Hawks. Georgia Bulldogs. My earliest memory was of my older brother Danny's obsession with University of Georgia running back Herschel Walker. Herschel this and Herschel that. And it wasn't just my brother. Every household in our area probably had a dog named Herschel.

I was five when my Bulldogs won the national championship in Walker's freshman year. This winning thing was easy. The recipe seemed so simple. Just add one superstar athlete, mix in a rabid fan base, and championships will start raining from the sky. Unfortunately for me, though, I was only five. Going to McDonald's for dinner and getting a happy meal toy would have been a bigger thrill for me back then. Although the sheer fact of that season left an indelible impression on me,

I couldn't really appreciate what was happening. At that point in my life there was no forty-year investment. I got more excited to watch Frosty the Snowman the one time it always came on before Christmas, than I did for a silly old college football game. What was college? What was football? However, my brother thought this was the biggest thing ever, so naturally, I did too. Thus began a forty-year love affair with sports. Forty years of hope, excitement, passion. Forty years of hanging on every pitch, every shot, every pass. And, unfortunately, forty years of anguish, heartache, and misery.

A funny thing happened on the way to "championships raining from the sky" ……the clouds dried up and the rain never came. Let me be the first to state the obvious. Yes, UGA did win the national championship in 1980. But just chew on this next thought for a minute. The Falcons franchise began play in 1966. No championships. The Atlanta Hawks moved from St. Louis in 1968. Since the move, no championships. The Atlanta Braves moved from Milwaukee in 1966 and we all are fully aware of the single, skinny championship in 1995. And, of course, UGA football has no national titles since that 1980 season. That equates to 200 seasons (we'll exclude the two NHL franchises, Flames and Thrashers, that made nary a whimper in their brief stints in our city). Let me repeat - one lonely, isolated championship for me and my fellow fanatics in 200 seasons (more on that one chip later).

For the moment, however, let's put collegiate sports aside and examine only the four major sports. By comparison, since 1966 (the year Atlanta emerged on the sports scene), Boston has 22 championships. New York has 21 championships. The Bay Area has combined for 18. Los Angeles has 17. Pittsburgh has surprisingly won 13. Chicago has 11. Detroit - 9. Philadelphia has at least one in each sport, winning a total of 7. Miami - 7. Dallas - 7.

Milwaukee/Green Bay has given Wisconsin fans 6 titles. Baltimore - 6. St. Louis – 6. Washington D.C. – 6. Denver – 5. For goodness sakes, even San Antonio, with only one professional franchise, has 5 championships. Kansas City has won 3. Houston was able to grab a couple when the Rockets won both years MJ was playing baseball, as well as a World Series title. Phoenix and Seattle have won in multiple sports, each winning 2. Our neighbors to the north have even gotten into the act, as Toronto has 3 non-hockey championships, while Montreal has 11 Stanley Cup victories.

Atlanta has one. Let me repeat that – Atlanta has exactly ONE championship. It is very true, one really is the loneliest number. Atlanta can collectively put on a giant foam finger, with the connotation of "we're number one" having all new meaning. It's so embarrassing, that most local fans tend to count franchise championships from other cities as their own. We rationalize the Milwaukee Braves' World Series victory in 1957 over the New York Yankees as a win in our ledger. Ditto for the St. Louis Hawks NBA title in 1958 over the Boston Celtics. I'm pretty sure I've said the word "we" when referencing those teams from Milwaukee and St. Louis. As in, WE beat the Yankees, or WE beat the Celtics. But can we please be honest with each other? They don't belong to us. They never have. They never will.

In case you fell asleep while reading that last paragraph, let me repeat – ONE championship for my teams in TWO HUNDRED seasons. That's a hard pill to swallow, but it is even tougher to take when you consider the opportunities they have had (and lost). Consider that the Braves have been to the playoffs 19 out of the last 28 seasons, the Falcons have reached multiple Super Bowls, UGA has knocked on the door of a title more than a handful of times, and the Hawks - well, never mind the

Hawks. Among those opportunities, there have been several titles so deeply within our grasp, I was already prepping my championship tattoo sleeve for the next commemorative ink job. Okay, I don't have a championship tattoo sleeve, but if I did, it would look pretty close to what it looks like now - empty.

    To be a sports fan, it takes a certain amount of blind loyalty. It takes following your team to the very end, even if the very end is bitter. I get it. I'm not asking to win in every sport, every season. I'm not expecting to come out victorious each time one my teams approaches the finish line. But come on! This is getting ridiculous. We've built up more angst than the U.S. government has national debt. Baseball has a saying that everything evens out in the end. If that's true, we have a lot of evening out to do. If the Curse of Tecumseh is indeed broken, we will have a glorious next fifty years, as we try and balance the books.

    Alas, nobody around here actually believes that will happen. We've been let down too many times. We've had our collective hopes risen to levels unimaginable, without the wins. The thing is, the higher the hopes, the harder the fall. None of us wants to fall anymore. We've been bruised, battered and beaten one too many times. Our psyches can't handle much more. For most cities, even after losing in the end, fan reflection is mostly full of fond memories of the journey. Well, I tell you, I'm tired of traveling. The view along the way to the ultimate destination is no longer of the scenic variety. Miley Cyrus once proclaimed, "it's the climb". No, it's not. At least, not for us anymore. It's about reaching the apex. The zenith. The acme. The top of the mountain. Or any other overused reference that implies achieving the pinnacle of success. I've finally gotten to the point where I have no desire to strap on my harness. I don't want to expend any more energy hiking up the mountain, when all that awaits me is the inevitable landslide.

I don't want to......but I will. We all will, because we can't help ourselves. I'm a statistics teacher by trade and these discussions come up regularly in classroom conversation. I tell my students every year to get out now. They are still young enough to change their path from sports fan to something else. Anything else. All that lies ahead of them is heartache from this wretched Curse. For me, and anyone else with so many years invested, we can't stop. It's too late for us. I tell my wife every time my heart gets ripped out, "No more!" or "That's it, I'm done!" I tell myself at the onset of each season to sit this one out. Sometimes, I actually make it a decent way through the course of the year. But somehow, I always find myself getting dragged back in. Instead of turning on THE game, in an effort to divert my attention, I may try to find something else interesting to watch. Occasionally, I might make it to the first commercial break without a thought of what's going on with the game. Invariably, I check the score. Let me tell you, checking a score is like smelling a piece of chocolate cake (insert apple pie, cinnamon roll, scone or whatever baked good suits your choosing). It's not long before you're devouring the entire thing. Sometimes, I wish I could go back to my days of innocence, when every season began fresh with hope of what may come.

Again, let me reiterate, it's not just that my teams lose. It's that they routinely find the most horrific, beyond-belief, that-should-never-have-happened-and-couldn't-possibly-happen-again, stick a fork in me now....... ways to lose. It was a mere three days after UGA won its national championship that the reality of who we were set back in. The Curse was ready to act. The Curse had giveth, now it was time to taketh away. In many regards, that 1980 title only served to make the next many years that much worse, because now we knew what ultimate success felt like. It was glorious. As a sports community, you are on top of the world. You are soaring with the eagles. And then………... you're not. Keep in mind, the Cubs and Red Sox were two of baseball's earliest dynasties before their curses took shape. I imagine winning those championships early on made their forthcoming droughts much less palatable. We can certainly sympathize.

At age 5, I had somehow also been roped into being a tag-along Falcons fan. My dad was a regular at the Falcons' training facility, The Complex, as we called it. He would work out in the fitness center, alongside many of my football heroes. Steve Bartkowski. William Andrews. Lynn Cain. My brother, in truth, was the real fan, but I always went along for the ride. While he was busy getting autographs, I was busy visiting the vending machine and the Pac-Man Arcade. These Falcons were good, though. Really good. Certainly, they were one of the up-and-coming teams in the league. With the echo of Larry Munson's gravelly voice calling UGA's romp to the championship still ringing in our ears, we were riding high. Up next, Super Bowl.

Not so fast. In true Atlanta fashion, the Falcons jumped all over their opponent, the Dallas Cowboys, early and often during their divisional round playoff game on January 4, 1981. In complete control of the game, they were up 24-10 entering the fourth quarter. The next fifteen minutes of the game, however, could be any fifteen minutes from a conveyor belt of games over the next 40 years. When the dust settled, the Falcons had blown the lead, which was still 10 points with just six minutes remaining. The Cowboys comeback was complete after a touchdown with just 42 seconds left, scoring 20 in the fourth quarter. Right about now you're probably thinking, *Wait a second! That could have happened to any team, in any given year.* Very true. But, consider this. If I gave you a single dollar, you have a dollar. No big deal. However, if I give you a dollar ten million times, you're rich. That's what it's like rooting for who I root for. Any one game like this, most would simply chalk it up to "not my day". But, when it occurs over and over and over again, it begins to take on a completely different meaning.

Losing one playoff game in this fashion should not be enough justification to label a sports town cursed. I wholeheartedly concur. However, when seemingly every high-stakes game, a natural platform for drama, ends with you holding your lifeless heart in the palm of your hands, then you have issues. Some would suggest that in order to even reach World Series or Super Bowls or National Championship games you must have had some great moments in high-stakes affairs. All true, but that's precisely how our Curse works. It builds you up and stokes your confidence to the point where you just know utter joy is right around the corner, before it is cruelly and callously yanked away. Yes, I've witnessed wins for the home team in big games. Plenty of them. However, those wins are seemingly always a precursor to an even bigger game, having bigger stakes, and accompanying an even bigger avalanche of disappointment.

Oh, and if that Falcons playoff debacle wasn't bad enough, the next season our star full back, William Andrews, blew out his knee and was never the same. Not just that, the loss to Dallas was an omen of things to come for the Falcons, as they would reach the playoffs only once over the next ten seasons.

Mid-Chapter Disclaimer: Read on only if you think you can stomach the horrors of what's to come. If you are squeamish in any way, I'd strongly advise you to reconsider any further torture. Rehashing the last forty years of our sports failures might put some of you in the fetal position. On the other hand, if you're not

from Georgia, it will surely make you appreciate what you have.

The Georgia Bulldogs had no sooner won the championship in 1980, then they were back at it again. However, this time Tecumseh began rearing his ugly head, as if to say, "let the rampage begin". Georgia was a great team. This team should really have won back-to-back-to-back titles. In 1981, the Bulldogs played the Clemson Tigers, in a game that would ultimately decide the national championship. Unfortunately, for the Bulldogs, their winning streak of 15 games was snapped in utterly ridiculous fashion, as they turned the ball over NINE times, losing 13-3. Seriously, nine turnovers. NINE. Five interceptions, four fumbles. I honestly can't remember UGA quarterback great Buck Belue ever throwing five passes in a GAME, much less five interceptions. Even Herschel himself fumbled it twice. Have you ever heard of such a thing? Nine giveaways! That's like saying you just ate nine Big Macs. Nobody would take you seriously. It just doesn't happen. But it did. You might watch a month's worth of games and not see that combined total. And, as you might remember, it was Clemson who went on to win the 1981 title. Georgia did not.

The 1982 season was no different. Georgia was very likely the best team in the country. They certainly had the best player, Herschel Walker, who was still breaking records into his Heisman Trophy-winning junior season. The Bulldogs made it all the way to bowl season as the top-ranked team in the country. All we had to do was defeat Penn State in the Sugar Bowl and we'd be champs once again. The favored Bulldogs, however, did not come through, as they lost 27-23, with the Nittany Lions' final score coming on a late 40-something-yard touchdown pass. If a late 40-something-yard touchdown pass sounds familiar, just wait another 35 years. It'll get much worse,

Bulldog fans. The Curse was just beginning to rev up its engines. Losing big games was still relatively new around here, mainly because we hadn't been in many of them. High stake losses were not as gut-punching as they are now. In many ways, we were really "just happy to be there".

Georgia had officially lost out on its chance to be something truly special. Herschel made off to the upstart USFL, forgoing his last year of eligibility for the greener pastures of professional football. You just don't replace a Herschel Walker and, of course, the Bulldogs did not. Unfortunately, Georgia wouldn't reach those heights again for quite some time. And when they did, well, you maybe wish they hadn't. But we'll get back to that conversation later.

As my childhood progressed, my love for sports began expanding. I had a new sports idol and his name was Dale Murphy, centerfielder for the Atlanta Braves. The first baseball season I remember was in 1982. And, as it happened, that was a magical year for my Braves. They won their first 13 games of the season. By any measure, that's a pretty good start. The Braves, for what it's worth, had not reached postseason play since losing to the Miracle Mets in 1969, so this run had been long-awaited. I fell in love with the team. I knew the lineup from top-to bottom, even still to this day.

My brother and I went outside nearly every summer day to play backyard baseball. Being the subservient younger sibling, I was usually forced into the batter's box, as my brother envisioned himself pitching through the Braves lineup. I was like Eddie Murphy in *Coming to America,* playing the role of every character. You should have seen me switching from one side of the batter's box to the next, dutifully batting lefthanded or righthanded, where appropriate. I was Brett Butler. Then, I was Claudell Washington. I was Dale Murphy, then Bob Horner, Chris Chambliss, and so on (I guess this is where I thank my brother for making me the great switch hitter I am today). That was my first summer of baseball and I was hooked. The Braves found themselves in a pennant race against the mighty and seasoned Los Angeles Dodgers. The defending World Series Champion Dodgers. The Dodgers of Fernando Valenzuela, Pedro Guerrero, Steve Garvey, and others. Somehow, the Braves fought the battle-tested Dodgers down to the very last day of the year, winning the division by a single game.

We were joyous and had nothing but the highest hopes for what the postseason had in store for us. In the NLCS, the Braves were up against the St. Louis Cardinals, the National League's most successful franchise and a team that will haunt the Braves in other postseasons to come. In my 7-year old mind, I didn't understand the Cardinals were probably the favored team. I mean, we had just ousted the defending champs - what could the Cardinals do to derail this train? I just knew Dale Murphy would carry us to the finish line on his way to the first of his two consecutive MVP seasons.

In Game One, we had future Hall of Famer Phil Niekro, the most successful knuckleballer in history, pitching for us. We had the Cardinals exactly where we wanted. In fact, Game One started exactly as we had hoped. The Braves were up 1-0 with one out in the bottom of the fifth inning, and Niekro was pitching a masterpiece. Every boy in Atlanta was already planning their next opportunity to practice tossing the knuckler. I know I was. Gaining the upper hand in a short five game series is huge, and the Braves were on the cusp of earning that advantage. Or so we thought. The Curse was looming and waiting to pounce. Just as the game was a mere two outs away from being official, the rains came. And came. So much so, that the game was postponed. Wait a second, I thought. What does postponed mean? I soon learned the rule that if a game gets called off before the losing team bats five times, it doesn't count. It doesn't count and nothing that had occurred in the game up to that point counted either. Not the 1-0 lead. Not Niekro's masterpiece. Not the momentum that accompanies a one game advantage.

    Every child is taught to never count your chickens before they hatch, but I am pretty sure I saw a few cracks in those shells. Our ace was on the mound, dazzling the opponent with a dancing and darting knuckleball. He probably could have gone out there for two more outs. My brother and I played in the rain all the time (in spite of our mom's protestations). Certainly, our best pitcher could find enough of a grip to make this game official. But Tecumseh was having none of that. The game WAS called. We did not have a one game lead. Even worse, Niekro was now burned for the next game, unable to play a part. When the Curse hits, it hits hard. As it turned out, the Cardinals won the new and improved Game One 7-0. Niekro returned for Game 2 and pitched another gem. Unfortunately, the bullpen blew the late 3-2 lead and we eventually lost. Game 3 was over quickly, as the Cards scored four in the second inning. And there it was. Just like that, the season was over. Had the rain held off for another 5 minutes, who knows what might have become of this series. But, it didn't. It never does.

    Entire book series could be written solely on the Braves' postseason failures and collapses, many of which we will detail later. However, this was MY first one and it hurt. Still, I knew the Braves were really good and would be back (silly me). Unfortunately, those Braves as we knew them, a team of such hope and promise, were essentially done. After a decent run at it again in '83 fell short, the wheels began to fall off rapidly. The Curse had its say, and it spoke loudly. Horner, the young phenom of a slugger, could not avoid injury and missed significant time. Then, once healthy, he bolted for mythical status in the Japanese league. The Braves traded away future all-stars Butler and Brook Jacoby to Cleveland for washed-up pitcher Len Barker (just one of MANY trades that have gone down in infamy around here), Niekro was traded away before reaching the age of retirement (not metaphorical retirement, but literal), aging reliever Bruce Sutter was signed to something like a thirty-year contract (that's right, I think we might still be paying him), and young hurler Pascual Perez somehow couldn't find the stadium (the circuitous I-285 was an issue for navigationally-challenged Pascual).

And just like that, all we had left was Dale Murphy. Thank goodness for Dale Murphy, but our two-time MVP couldn't carry the entire team on his shoulders alone. We wouldn't hear so much as a peep from the Braves for another eight years. Or, as I like to say, we gave the Curse a chance to take a sabbatical. Oh, and by the way, major league baseball eventually changed the rainout rule thirty years later (or thirty years too late), to say that all game progress will carry over to the next day. Of course, that doesn't do us any good now, does it?

As a city, trying to learn how to win on the biggest of stages was still something we hadn't yet figured out. But, hey, we were still getting our feet wet (sorry, pun intended). We were just beginning to dip our toe in the big boy pool of sports. We were still a young sports city, maturing, growing, and finding our own identity. Our professional teams had only been around for 16 years. We were still learning how to drive. We'll get there. These things take time. Surely, this curse thing isn't real. Right??

Chapter 3

No Joy In Mudville

The mid-to-late 1980's was sort of a black hole in sports for the locals. The Falcons were one of the worst franchises in the NFL. Top draft picks, year in and year out, never translated into anything fruitful. The Braves couldn't get out of their own way, with the only fireworks coming from the memorable Fourth of July game against the Mets in 1985. Even my hero, Dale Murphy, was beginning to fade prematurely by 1989. Georgia football was still in hangover mode from the glory days of the early 80's, never recovering from the missed opportunities. Eventually, the Dawgs looked to move Vince Dooley to management and hit the reset button (I'm going to let you in on a little secret - the reset didn't work).

The only real excitement in the house was a high-flying, bow-legged, dunking maniac out of the University of Georgia. Drafted by the Utah Jazz in 1982, Dominique Wilkins somehow magically made his way over to the Atlanta Hawks. There was not a kid in the state of Georgia who wasn't in awe of the "Human Highlight Film", as Wilkins was known. The moniker says it all. He was human, yet he was also a freakishly athletic highlight reel. Those Hawks had stockpiled a deep stable of young talent, but talent was everywhere in the NBA glory days of the 1980's.

My Hawks won 50 games every season, but there was always a better team standing in the way. The Milwaukee Bucks. The Detroit Pistons. And, of course, those Larry Bird-led Boston Celtics. It was those Celtics who had won the Eastern Conference each year from 1984-1987. Who would supplant them when their run was over? Would it be the feisty Bucks, who seemed to be in the mix every year? Michael Jordan and his Bulls were still a little green around the edges to have any real say on the matter. The Pacers and Cavaliers were certainly on the rise. Would it be those Bad Boy Pistons? Or would it be us? In truth, there was no real discernable difference between those Hawks and Pistons teams. We each had a superstar (the Pistons had the plucky Isiah Thomas), with plenty of talented complimentary pieces surrounding them. In 1987, the Pistons had the first crack at the Celtics in the Eastern Conference playoffs, only to have Larry Bird steal away the game and the series. But in 1988, it was our turn. In the semifinals, the Hawks had the Celtics dead to rights. Up three games to two, with Game Six at home. The Hawks have not had many big moments in their forty-plus seasons in Atlanta, but this was definitely one of them. The Curse had already touched UGA, it had devoured the Falcons, and it had crippled the Braves. Hopefully, these Hawks would be different.

Earlier that season, perhaps as a bit of foreshadowing, Wilkins and Michael Jordan took flight in the most memorable dunk contest of all time. The two best rim-rattlers in the NBA were dueling it out, mano-a-mano. Wilkins was throwing down vicious tomahawk slams and unparalleled windmill dunks. Jordan was kissing-the-rim and jumping from the free throw line. It was epic. From our vantage point, Dominique was the clear winner. Even among NBA aficionados, Wilkins won the contest. However, the event was held in Chicago, in Jordan's home arena. Of course it was. Isn't it always? The NBA in the 80's was first and foremost a marketing machine. Could you imagine the outcry if Jordan had lost on his own home court? The fans booing and hissing, with Dominique Wilkins hoisting the trophy. No way they were going to let that happen. Or should I say, no way the Curse was going to let that happen. Jordan was awarded the victory, on his way to international icon status, while Wilkins was sent packing back to Atlanta, with only his dignity and pride to carry back with him. Wilkins was a quiet warrior. He probably wasn't the best player in the league, but he was our best. The dunk contest seems like a nonsensical thing to be consternated about, but consider the sports landscape in Atlanta at that time. Dominque was all we had. This contest meant everything. In our minds, it would spotlight our town to the nation. It would let everybody around the country know that we had arrived. This was our moment. This was our chance to put Atlanta on the sports map. And this was our guy, doing what he does best.

But……. this was Atlanta. William Tecumseh Sherman said it best, when he referred to his campaign as "total war". Nothing gets left intact. Nothing is left untouched. Total destruction and decimation. Why would a "meaningless" slam dunk contest be any different? It wasn't. The fact that vertically-challenged sensation Spud Webb and Wilkins had won other dunk contests meant very little. This was the one we wanted. Dominique vs. Jordan. The Human Highlight Film vs. His Airness. However, the increasingly all-too-familiar scent of coming up short was filling the room. It was to be an odor that would fill many rooms in Atlanta over the next generation of sporting events.

Fast-forward approximately three months and there we sat. The Hawks needing just a single win to vanquish the mighty Celtics and write their names in history as the team that dethroned Bird, McHale, Parrish, et al. Game Six. At home. Raucous crowd. The Celtics were anything but vintage Celtics on this night. They tried everything they could to give us the game. Boston only made two field goals in the last five-plus minutes. Turnovers left and right, but the Hawks ultimately could not capitalize on their opportunities. Still, with five seconds left, down by two, we had Wilkins, the ball and a chance. Just get the ball to Wilkins and all may be saved. Just get the ball to Wilkins and we may walk off the court having secured the biggest victory in Atlanta sports history. Just get the ball to……. Cliff Levingston?? That's right, the last shot went to bench player Cliff Levingston, who was only able to muster an off-balanced, wrong-handed shot that wasn't even close. To me, this is what separates champions from non-champions. Larry Bird would have gotten that final shot. Michael Jordan would have gotten that final shot. Not Cliff Levingston. You do what it takes to make sure your one superstar has the ball in his hands with the game on the line. Not us. Not on this night. Tecumseh had to be laughing in his grave. In the end, the Celtics won the game 102-100, on Atlanta's home court, nonetheless.

Even Larry Bird said we had our chance and we blew it. He was right. Game Seven would switch venues, the series moving back to Boston. If you know anything about sports history, you know good and well that almost nobody comes into the Boston Garden and beats the Celtics. Were we really expecting anything different? Our opportunity to close this thing out in our city, in front of our fans, had come and gone. Now, we had to go back to Boston and try to do the impossible. Was our franchise, our city, really going to be the one to do what other teams have not? In case you haven't noticed yet, we are not that city.

As it turned out, Game Seven was a thriller. Aren't they always? Our superstar Wilkins was not going to let us lose. He was magnificent. He was going to strap us all on his back and carry us to the Promised Land. Unfortunately, Larry Bird was thinking the same thing. And, as we saw, Bird's back apparently could carry a little more weight. Dominique was unconscious, shooting an unheard of 19-23 from the floor, scoring 47 points. He was trying to "will" his team to victory. However, Bird's "will" must have been made of titanium. He, too, was not about to let his team lose. Just like in the dunk contest against Jordan, Wilkins was again going mano-a-mano against one of the NBA elite. But this time it wasn't only Wilkins vs. Larry Legend. It was Atlanta vs. Boston. It was 0 championships vs. 16 championships. Ultimately, it was the Curse vs. the Shamrock. The fourth quarter was insane, with Wilkins and Bird going back and forth in perhaps the greatest one-on-one duel in basketball history. Wilkins was throwing up crazy bank shots, while Bird was tossing in lefthanded leaners. Wilkins' acrobatics pitted against Bird's effortless jumper. Not one person could lay blame on Wilkins if the Hawks were to lose this one. Bird, for his part, scored 20 in the fourth quarter alone. In the end, just like in Game Six, the Celtics came away with the narrowest of two-point wins. Of course they did. They always do. The Curse lives on.

    I was crushed. Not the Hawks, too? Is every duel going to come down to our heroic superstar coming up just short in the end? Emphatically, YES! Those Hawks of the 80's ended up just like all our other teams of that generation, on the wrong side of the Curse and on the scrapheap of what-might-have-beens. They never recovered from that series. The Pistons were eventually the team to supplant the Celtics. We even aided in their venture. In 1989, the Pistons offered our backup center Jon Koncak a one-year, $2.5 million contract to jump from the Hawks over to their side. Most Hawks fans were thrilled. We were still upset that we had selected Koncak number five overall in the 1985 draft, ahead of names such as Hall of Famers Chris Mullin or Karl Malone. Even Detlef Schrempf or Manute Bol would have been an upgrade. Heck, there were at least twenty players I would rather the Hawks have chosen. In my house, we said to let him go. I'm sure we weren't alone. But the Hawks did not let him go. Instead, they offered Koncak a six-year, $13 million dollar deal that he gladly accepted. More than Magic Johnson. More than Larry Bird. More than Michael Jordan. Are you kidding me? Most of us believed the Pistons were simply playing a high-risk game of chicken with the Hawks, knowing that if the Hawks bit, they would be severely hindering their own salary structure. The Pistons' gamble paid off and the Hawks signed the player who became known as Jon "Contract".

The Pistons became two-time champions, while the Hawks, behind their new high-priced backup center wallowed in mediocrity. To rub our faces in the dirt a little, Wilkins wasn't even invited to join the famed Dream Team for the 1992 Olympics in Barcelona. By all measures, he should have been one of the twelve. Even his peers agreed. But the one that mattered disagreed. No, I don't mean NBA Commissioner David Stern. I'm referring to the one that truly mattered, the Curser himself, Tecumseh. Instead of Wilkins, the Dream Team chose college star Christian Laettner. Let's see now, Dominique Wilkins vs. Christian Laettner. That doesn't have the same ring to it as 'Nique vs. Jordan, or 'Nique vs. Bird. Yet again, Wilkins came out on the short end of that stick as well.

These Hawks did, however, have one last shot at redemption. In 1994, the Hawks were leading the Eastern Conference at the halfway point of the season. Michael Jordan was off playing baseball, giving every team in the league new life. It was no different for the Hawks. The key piece, our future Hall of Famer Dominique Wilkins, was still there doing his thing. This just may be the year, or so we all thought. Out of nowhere, on February 24, 1994 (a date that lives on in Atlanta sports infamy), the Hawks traded their top scorer, team leader, and fan favorite Wilkins to the Los Angeles Clippers for Danny Manning. What? Danny Manning was great during his college years at Kansas, especially during their magical run in 1988, but really? Danny Manning for Dominique Wilkins? This felt anything but equitable. Who trades their best player during the season in which they are leading the league? Why would you trade your superstar, when this is your first real shot (perhaps the last shot) of glory in so many years? We couldn't believe it.

The phrase "only in Atlanta" was just in its infancy, but it was beginning to take on a life of its own. As in, only in Atlanta will a playoff game get rained out, with your team winning and only two outs to go. This time it was, only in Atlanta will a team forfeit its chances at a title by trading away the franchise for a chronically injured, never-lived-up-to-all-the-hype, fringe all-star from out west. The season was doomed from that point on. The Hawks, as expected, flamed out in the playoffs and never recovered. Danny Manning was gone by the next season through free agency after only 26 games as a Hawk. Simply put, we traded Dominique Wilkins, by far the greatest player in our franchise's history, for 26 games of Danny Manning. Unfathomable. But, as I said, only in Atlanta. Those Hawks of my youth, the Hawks of Dominique Wilkins, were gone.

To make matters worse, the Hawks proceeded to have the most woeful draft record in the NBA. The best player drafted by the Hawks from 1986 to 2006 was probably Stacey Augmon. Let's repeat that. In a span of twenty years, the best player the Hawks could come up with was Stacey Augmon, "Plastic Man" himself. Well, I guess we did draft All-Star Pau Gasol. Unfortunately, he was the one draft pick we decided to trade away before even suiting up for the Hawks. Lottery picks included the likes of the aforementioned Koncak, Rumeal Robinson, DerMarr Johnson, Josh Childress, Acie Law, Marvin Williams and Shelden Williams. Yikes. Typical Atlanta. Scouting? Who needs it? That has to be considered the most inept draft legacy of any franchise, in any sport. I challenge anyone to come up with anything close.

    Cynicism was now setting in for all of us in the ATL. Perhaps, those three letters ATL stood for All Teams Lose? None of this made much sense to my still-impressionable mind. Atlanta had taken on the nickname "Loserville" and for good reason. The Curse was picking up steam.

Chapter 4

Prime Time…For A While Anyway

The 1990's were here. The teams of the 80's, Dodgers and Cardinals and Athletics, Lakers and Celtics and Pistons, 49ers and Giants and Redskins and Bears, were all wrapping up a decade of dominance. So, the last ten years didn't go so well for my teams. I was still young. I was still brimming with hope and optimism. For all I knew, the next ten years would bring a windfall of championships. It could happen. Or, so I thought.

The Falcons had a rough go of it since their last foray into the playoffs in 1982, but in 1989 they actually got a draft pick right. With the fifth overall pick, the Falcons selected Deion Sanders, "Prime Time" as he was self-proclaimed. To all of us, he was everything he said he was. Our team had a star, a player that even fans outside of Atlanta wanted to watch. All eyes were on Sanders. Every time he touched the ball, or even had a chance to touch it, there was electricity in the air.

To have a player like that on your team is a rare commodity, at least for my teams. To see him run back a punt is like watching Michael Jackson moonwalk. You know they are doing things differently, yet better than anyone else who has ever tried. My brothers and I (and every other teenage boy) would play football in the back yard, galloping down the imaginary sideline, trying to glide just like Neon Deion. If you are questioning my enthusiasm for Sanders, I simply ask you to Google some old footage of him returning kicks or picks, and tell me it's not the most wonderful thing you have seen. This is the kind of player we had been clamoring for, a superstar who could not only talk the talk, but always walked the walk. He did it all – intercepted passes, returned kicks, played a little receiver, and, oh yeah, a little baseball, as well. While he was dancing on the field, MC Hammer (a huge Falcons fan for some reason, despite famously being from Oakland) was dancing on the sidelines.

For a couple of seasons, we had a little bubble of excitement. All we needed was a true star quarterback, not the delicately-boned Chris Miller. Then, in 1991, we drafted him. We drafted a true superstar. We drafted a future Super Bowl Winner and MVP. We drafted a future Hall of Famer. The only problem is, he was none of those things for us. You might not remember, but the Falcons were the team that drafted Brett Favre. Yes, THAT Brett Favre. Unfortunately, he only lasted one year in Atlanta. The Falcons traded him away the following year to the Packers for a couple of footballs. Okay, we actually traded Favre for the 19th pick of the draft, but that selection became running back Tony Smith. For some reason, it makes the trade seem a little less lopsided to say the return was equipment. Favre was out of here in a flash, leaving us in the dust on his way to Super Bowl glory.

Two years after Favre was traded, our charismatic superstar Sanders was on his way out as well. He signed to play with the hated San Francisco 49ers. Of all the teams, did it have to be the 49ers, the one team that had caused us the most feelings of heartache and inferiority? Not only that, he was awesome for them, winning Defensive Player of the Year. And in typical "Prime Time" fashion, he returned to the Georgia Dome for the first time, bringing with him all of the fanfare and smack talk you would have expected. To his credit, he performed, as it seemed like he always did. I always admired that element of clutchness he seemed to possess, an element that was so sorely lacking among our teams. Neon Deion returned to his former house and did so in grand fashion, returning a 93-yard interception for a touchdown against his former team. In truth, even though he was on the other sideline this time, we loved it. We enjoyed the high-stepping, taunting, don't-you-wish-you-still-had-me dash down the field. Later that year, Sanders and the 49ers won the Super Bowl.

It's not that stars had never graced our town, it's that they were usually on the other team. And if they WERE on our own team, back then it seemed as though it was only a matter of time before they'd be elsewhere. See Brett Favre. See Deion Sanders. I always have liked the phrase "the devil is in the details". It's the little things that are the most problematic. That's what makes the Curse so frustrating for all of us. It's so many little things, piled one on top of the other, that have become this mountain of sports calamity.

Details like drafting players. The Hawks couldn't find a single player in TWO DECADES. The Falcons did draft star players, only to see them win big for other teams. The word "draft" became like a profane four-letter word in our household. There were only the lowest of the low expectations. Names like Dallas Comegys, Roy Marble, Priest Lauderdale, Adam Keefe, oh, and Jon Koncak went up on the Hawks draft board year after year. This list of has-beens, also-rans, and never-weres just kept growing and growing. Top 10 picks that nobody had heard of and haven't since. Even the Falcons, who at least had some real successes in the draft (for other teams' benefit, unfortunately), selected linebacker Aundray Bruce (Yikes!) with the first pick in 1988. Remember him? I didn't think so. Draft nights were a veritable horror show. Year after year. All of our general managers and executives suffered from the same malady. They were averse to getting it right. All of them, except one.

Of all the managerial decisions I questioned from the Braves' Bobby Cox, and there were MANY, one thing is definitely unquestioned. He was an outstanding general manager, especially in talent evaluation, which included drafting. After managing the Blue Jays to the playoffs, Cox was tasked to rebuild the Braves from the muck that was the 80's. He is a Hall of Fame manager, but in reality, he was a Hall of Fame GM. All of that talent that made him so successful in the dugout was actually procured by him as a general manager. And he was tremendous. Names like Tom Glavine, John Smoltz, Ron Gant, David Justice, Steve Avery and, of course, Larry Wayne "Chipper" Jones Jr. were all a product of Cox the GM. He drafted the right players (Jones), traded for the right players (Smoltz) and retained the right players from the previous regime (Glavine). From 1985-90 he seemingly made all the right moves. He did trade away Dale Murphy to the Phillies for no return players of significance and signed slugger Nick Esasky, who never made an impact due to an infamous case of vertigo, but otherwise was flawless. In truth, trading away Murphy was a sentimental blow, but he was effectively done by that time.

The Falcons continued their history of flubs and missteps into the 90's, the Hawks were annually the definition mediocrity, and the talent-rich Georgia Bulldogs were on the fast track to becoming the Florida Gators' doormat. The Curse was humming right along, but the Braves were ready to challenge its dominance

The Atlanta Braves of the 80's were more or less the *NSYNC of baseball. The musical group was basically seen as lead singer Justin Timberlake (Yes, I know, a second JT reference) and everyone else. Well, so were the Braves. Dale Murphy was the lead singer, doing his best to get the fans out of their seats, while the other Braves were his background dancers. In pop music, that's a recipe for Billboard Top 100 gold. Unfortunately, in baseball, that sort of construction earns you the basement of the National League year in and year out. But all that changed in 1991. The Curse of Tecumseh had better get its act together or the Braves were going to make a mockery out of it. Atlanta was amassing quite the squad, as Bobby Cox had been stockpiling fresh talent over the last few years. That talent was now ready to crash onto the big stage.

Chapter 5

Had We Only Known Then...

The 1991 season started innocently enough, but even .500 baseball was a huge deal for Braves fans, considering they were an abysmal last place team the previous year(s). But these Braves were maturing rapidly, improving daily. Sprinkle in some well-timed veteran additions (Terry Pendleton, Sid Bream come to mind), and the team was primed and ready. Just as in 1982, the good guys battled down to the very last weekend of the year against the Dodgers. This time Los Angeles brought with them old friend and now all-star Brett Butler, serving as a reminder of what Atlanta had missed out on the last ten years. We all suspected the Braves might not quite yet be ready. But they were. They defeated the Dodgers in a dramatic pennant chase, making the playoffs for the first time since that '82 season.

I'll never forget that Saturday afternoon in October, watching as the Braves clinched. Atlanta winning their game against the Astros securing a division tie, famously sending catcher Greg Olson into the arms of victorious John Smoltz (remember when pitchers actually threw complete games?). Then, watching the Braves players remain on the field to watch the final inning of the Dodgers-Giants game on the big screen. The Dodgers lost. Let the jubilation begin.

In this moment of reflection, let me be honest. Nothing in my lifetime has come close to the delirium that surrounded Atlanta during that baseball season. All ages, from the very youngest to the very eldest, had suddenly become Braves fanatics. I can remember everybody coming to work or school bleary-eyed, after having stayed up to the wee hours, as the Braves played late-season west coast games. An entire city turned on its head. Perhaps, because the season had come out of nowhere. For whatever reason, this season, this team, this experience resonated with the entire community. Nobody wanted to be "Loserville" any longer. We needed this and we relished every moment.

I vividly recall being in our car during one particular Sunday afternoon September game against those Dodgers, a game the Braves won. As the final out took place, we just happened to be at a stoplight. What ensued could only be described as beautiful, spontaneous joy. At that little stoplight in Loganville, Georgia the celebration began. Every car horn started honking victoriously. I remember looking out the window to my left and seeing the lady in the next car tomahawk chopping. The car behind us had choppers, as well. It was so exciting celebrating at the traffic light with complete strangers. For one moment, we were all the same. There was no black or white, no male or female, no young or old. We were all Atlanta Braves fans. We were bonded in a way that few things could.

They had gone from worst to first, the tagline that had become so chic during the season, referencing both the Braves and the American League's Minnesota Twins. In the NLCS, nobody really expected the Braves to do much. They were party crashers, trying to ruin the inevitable coronation of the highly-touted Pittsburgh Pirates. The Pirates of the Killer B's, specifically Bobby Bonilla and young Barry Bonds. Pittsburgh had reached this same point last year, but had come up short. In their mind, and everybody else's, it was their year. It sure seemed like it, as they took a 3-2 series lead. Bravo Braves! You did well to get this far, but it's time to go home and let the big boys play on.

Once, when I was an eighth grader, some of us basketballers were playing a little pickup game in the gym after school. The varsity team wanted to get us runts off the floor, as they did on every other day. But as pickup game rules have gone since time began, you have to get beat to get run off the court. On this day, neither I, nor my teammates, were going to get beat. My little eighth graders kept winning. And winning. I was on fire. We all were. It was a great feeling. I wanted it to last as long as possible, and although I was going to give every ounce of effort, I knew eventually the big boys were going to win. The Braves were like us eighth graders. They didn't want to get off the court. They also probably knew the big boys (Pirates) wanted to brush them off, but they were going to scratch and claw to the very end. Games 6 and 7, in Pittsburgh, mind you, saw the young Braves send a 21- and 24-year old, respectively, to the mound. Those young guns were Steve Avery and John Smoltz. And you know what? Those baby-faced assassins proceeded to shut out the favored Pirates in back-to-back games. The Pirates were never able to run these party crashers off the court.

The Braves had won the series. The Curse was broken. Finally, a win in the spotlight moment. It was an amazing feeling. All those years of coming so close, but not closing the deal, were gone. My family celebrated with reckless abandon, as you would expect in a house with three teenage boys. We had done what had seemed so impossible. My Braves were the ones to look the Curse in the face and laugh. They had crossed the finish line.

Only they hadn't. The celebration in our house was something akin to a sprinter raising his hands in exultation, only to have an even grittier runner put his head down and catch you in the end. Cue the Minnesota Twins. Cue the grittier runner. Cue the Curse.

The Curse has only grown to full maturity in recent years. Back in 1991, we really didn't understand the nuances of what it meant to be cursed. What if those 1981 Falcons had actually not blown the late lead to the Cowboys? What if they had reached the Super Bowl, only to lose to the eventual champion Oakland Raiders? Would we have been less heartbroken? We thought the Braves losing to the Cardinals in '82 was tough. What if they had beaten the Cards, then lost in the World Series to the Milwaukee Brewers? Would that have been easier to swallow? What if, instead of losing to the Celtics in the Eastern Conference playoffs, the Hawks had beaten them, only to lose in the NBA Finals to the Los Angeles Lakers? Would we have remembered that season more fondly? We had it backwards. We had it easy. Losing early had actually been saving us from a more terrible side of the Curse. The side that makes you think you might win it all. The side that prepares the engraving materials for your name on the trophy. Queen's rock anthem didn't cry out "We Are *Almost* the Champions".

The Curse was beginning to progress. Initially, it allowed us to only go so far. We were a young sports city. Our hearts probably couldn't have taken more than what we went through. But now, we had experienced some ups and some downs as a sports community, and the Curse, accordingly, was upping its game. It's like giving a toddler a tricycle. The training wheels are there for the child's protection, but at some point, they get removed and replaced with a bicycle. After growing and learning how to pop a wheelie, you may reach the Moped stage. Eventually, though, at full maturation, you are ready for the motorcycle, the Big Hog itself. For the Atlanta-Athens sports contingent, in 1991, we had reached the bicycle stage of the Curse. They say every growth period is hard. Having three children now myself, I will agree to this point. But, I'm not sure we were even close to being prepared for what was about to happen.

The city had reached a new level of investment with these Braves. And, as I stated before, the higher your hopes, the harder the fall. We certainly had not been this hopeful for the Braves. The excitement in every sector of our community was palpable, almost tangible. The Curse was probably licking its chops, as if to tell us all "Look out below!"

The World Series against the Minnesota Twins has gone down in history as, perhaps, the most exciting, thrilling series ever. As I say, aren't they always. A good sports curse gives you the expected loss. However, ours is a GREAT sports curse. Not only do we lose, we lose in some of the most harrowing, stomach-churning, I-need-a-heart-defibrillator ways. Even though we know the curse is omnipresent, when we get so tantalizingly close to victory, we can't help but fall prey to false hope.

Society teaches us that it is always darkest before the dawn. But the Curse teaches a different lesson. We have been students at the feet of the Curse, like ancient Greeks sitting around Socrates, getting fed knowledge of its ways. The Curse demonstrates time and again the dawn will never come. If anything, the dawn comes first. What do you call beating the Dodgers in an amazing race to the division title? What do you consider reviving ourselves and completing the comeback against the Pirates? Those were anything, but "dark" moments. Those WERE "the dawn", and the darkness was still to come.

But, of course, we didn't know all of this then. We have learned our lessons well over the years, but we were just entering middle school of the Curse Academy back in 1991. We were still in our awkward phase, just trying to find our identity in the sports world. Nothing was set in stone. The book on us had not been fully written. Our future was still ahead of us and it (potentially, but not in actuality) could have been bright.

We entered the series with the Twins expecting the best. After two narrow losses, however, our countenance had dampened a little. The most memorable moment was in Game 2, which saw Minnesota's archvillain Kent Hrbek lifting Ron Gant's leg off first base, recording the out and stifling a pivotal Braves rally. Every moment always seems to be pivotal and there ALWAYS seems to be a Kent Hrbek lurking. This may be a good time to point out that Gant was actually safe. Why is instant replay never around when you need it? I'm sure even Hrbek, himself, didn't think the umpire would actually call Gant out. I imagine first basemen all around the world tried to impersonate Hrbek's move after it worked IN THE WORLD SERIES. Why not? It turned out to be a huge turning point, as the game was still tied into the eighth inning. However, light-hitting Twin infielder Scott Leius was able to muster a little Minnesota magic and hit a go-ahead homer in the bottom of the inning off 1991 Cy Young Award winner and future Hall Of Famer Tom Glavine. Twins won 3-2.

I now realize there will always be a Scott Leius, as well. Ours was Mark Lemke, the scrappy second baseman who outperformed his ability every postseason. The problem is, it is impossible to out-Scott Leius Scott Leius himself. Just the name sends shivers down my spine. Scott Leius? Really? The man had only five home runs the entire season, only 28 for his entire career. 28! Yet, in this moment he wasn't merely Scott Leius, he was SCOTT

LEIUS. Most people remember the Hrbek play and rightfully so. It was such a turning point play, Minnesota produced a bobblehead in 2011 commemorating the play and the twentieth anniversary of the 1991 World Series. Of course, they did. Without the Hrbek play, there is a better-than-decent chance the Braves score that inning and likely win the game. But, for me, the ultimate deciding blow was the Leius homer. If you ask Glavine what single pitch he would want back from his career, I guarantee you it would be that one.

It would have been so easy to have crumbled against the veteran Twins and let them waltz to a ho-hum series victory. However, we have a savage Curse. It doesn't want to defeat you, it wants to cut your heart out with a spoon. It wants total surrender. Considering this, it should be to no one's surprise that the Braves came back to win the next three games back home in Atlanta, mostly in dramatic fashion. But the series was shifting back to that haunted house in Minnesota, the Metrodome. It should be noted that in the 1987 Series the Twins took all four games against the Cardinals at the Metrodome as well. So, the Twins still had visions of success, but so did we. How cute. Who were we kidding?

With the Braves up 3-2, who knew that this already thriller of series was about to get historic? Who knew that names like Puckett, Leibrandt, Morris, and Lonnie Smith were about to be immortalized as either the G.O.A.T. or a goat? It's a fine line between champ and chump. All athletes (along with their fans) walk the tightrope between victory and misery. In a game of inches, you never know which way the winds of destiny will blow. Except, this is Atlanta. We should have had a pretty good idea of what was about to happen.

Cox gets a lot of grief for bringing in Leibrandt in that fateful Game Six, as well he should. That was a terrible decision. He is the only manager in history that would have gone to Leibrandt in that situation, and we saw why. The Curse doesn't need any help and Bobby Cox, very often, seemed like Tecumseh's covert agent, sabotaging from within. Sometimes, though, you get beat by a great player like Kirby Puckett. He put his team on his back and almost singlehandedly tied the series. Truthfully, even if we disregard the Game Six debacle, the Braves should have won Game Seven.

It seemed as though we were always one play away from making Jack Morris blink first in that historic Game Seven duel between him and John Smoltz. Case in point, examine the top of the eighth. Atlanta's Lonnie Smith was on first base with no outs, when Terry Pendleton doubled into the gap. Pendleton, the league MVP that season, had come up with big hit after big hit all year for the Braves, and he came through again here in the biggest of situations. Clutch Pendleton was the man we wanted at the plate in that moment, and he delivered the Braves a 1-0 lead with only six outs separating the Braves from the championship. At least, that's what should have happened. Oh, Pendleton got the hit, alright. However, Lonnie Smith, who should have been getting congratulatory high fives from his dugout, was still standing on third base. What? How?

It turns out, Smith forgot to look at his third base coach, as every little leaguer is taught. Instead, he looked at Twins shortstop Greg Gagne as he approached second base. Greg Gagne? Yep, he looked at right Gagne's weak attempt to decoy the the baserunner. At least, to all other baserunners in the history of baseball, it would have been considered a weak attempt. A terrible, half-hearted acting job. But, to Smith, it was worthy of an Academy Award. He bit. Stopping at second for what seemed like minutes, until he finally spotted the ball in the outfield. Smith was only able to make it around to third base. Let's get this straight – if Smith spots his third base coach, as he has done thousands of times, we win the World Series? That's right. But you guessed it, he did not. Thanks Curse!

Sports is littered with names of players that became synonymous with being a goat (and I don't mean G.O.A.T., as in Greatest Of All Time). Unfortunately, Lonnie Smith added his name to this list. Unfortunately for him, for his team, for his city. It was also unfortunate that his nickname was "Skates", so-named for the way he looked when he ran the bases, like he was on skates. I had been a huge Lonnie Smith fan up to that point. After Game 7, however, all I remembered was the appropriateness of his nickname and how his baserunning blew our chances in 1991.

Now, it is absolutely unfair to completely blame Smith for not scoring. We still, after all, had runners on second and third with no outs. After a walk to Justice to load the bases, Ron Gant grounded out to first, then Sid Bream hit into an inning-ending double play. However, it is much easier to forgive physical errors, rather than mental ones. Thus, Smith gets the lion's share of the culpability. In the end, the Braves did NOT score. The Twins won the game. Jack Morris became legend. The Curse lived on.

Anyone that says baseball is a slow-paced three-hour bore fest, clearly, has never watched a postseason game. Every pitch, every swing, every umpire call, every managerial decision has something riding on it. Your heart is in your throat from the first moment to the last. This series, though, took things to a different level. There was a moment in Game Seven, with Pendleton's double shooting into the gap, that had an entire fan base jumping out of their seats. And for a brief moment, every single one of us had the thought, "We're about to win the World Series". AND

THERE IT IS! That's precisely what makes The Curse of Tecumseh so deliciously diabolical. As we have seen time and time again in our town, there is inevitably that single moment when we all arise as one and say, "That's it! We've won!". This game was no different than our other big games before, except that it was the final game. There would be no more, under any conditions. That simple fact makes the end result so much more excruciating. The chance to win it all was right before you, and you let it slip through your hands. You think back to every Kent Hrbek moment, every Scott Leius moment and, certainly, every Lonnie Smith moment and wonder what might have been. Now, we look back at the Cowboys game of '81, the Cardinals series of '82, and the Celtics series of '88 and acknowledge how much easier those losses were. Easier to go through, and definitely easier to get over. Little did we know this series was going to be a microcosm of the next 28 years.

    We blamed Kent Hrbek. We blamed the umpires. We blamed Lonnie Smith. We blamed Charlie Leibrandt. We blamed Bobby Cox. But, if we had been cognizant of what actually was going down, we would have ultimately blamed the Curse. In the end, because this was our first exposure to professional championship competition, we were still proud of our team. In fact, the city put on a championship-style parade that could have rivaled any other. Now, I've never really heard of a celebration for coming in second. But that's exactly what we did. I'll admit, I wanted to go and "celebrate" with the rest of the city. I look back on it now, though, and ask, "What were we thinking?" Having a parade after LOSING the World Series is like celebrating coming up one number short of winning the Power Ball. Who does that? We do. That's a sad referendum on the sports landscape of our fair city, when we are reduced to celebrating our status as the runner-up. I can't imagine that happening nowadays. We've been down that road to "almost, but not quite" too many times.

Interestingly, one my favorite movies growing up was *The Best of Times,* starring Robin Williams. The film centers around a former high school football has-been, who lives in a supposedly cursed town, trying to relive his "almost-but-not-quite" moment. The protagonist, Williams, had never recovered from bringing defeat out of certain victory in the big game, having been solely responsible for their curse living on. For his town, that was their moment, and he fumbled it away in devastating fashion. The burden of it all weighed him down like an anchor around his neck. It had been 13-plus years since that game, yet the curse, as well as his part in it, was all too much to bear. He couldn't rest until redemption was had.

I was always fascinated by the movie, years before I had any notion of a sports curse in my own town. The film encapsulates every feeling, every emotion that sports fans in my area have felt for years. What is it going to take to break the Curse? Is it even possible? The weight is felt by us all. The fans feel it. The teams feel it. The city feels it. We're lying to ourselves (fans and players, alike) if we say we don't feel that extra amount of pressure resulting from the Curse. Routine plays become a little tougher. Game-changing moments become a little more anxious. No matter how great we are playing, there is always that little voice in our head saying, "when is the other shoe going to drop?" And so far, it almost always has. We know that feeling, that voice, very well. Usually, the familiar is comforting. Not in this case. This familiarity breeds distress and angst. At film's end, Robin Williams, his team, and his city broke their curse. For some ridiculous reason, that gives me hope. Perhaps, one day, Tecumseh will say "enough", and the curse will be lifted.

Chapter 6

At Least We Got One

The 1991 season had come and gone. Yet, the Braves were about to take center stage as lead characters in one of the most dramatic soap operas. A show that, unfortunately for the Braves, will last almost three decades. The 1992 season was different, if for no other reason than the Braves were now a known quantity and they were expected to win. I know I expected it. The regular season was not nearly as intense as the previous, as Braves won the division by a comfortable eight games. As a bonus, Atlanta superstar Deion Sanders was now doing his two-sport thing here. Dynamically patrolling the outfield for the Braves during the week, "Prime Time" was simultaneously strutting into endzones for the Falcons on Sundays. It was exciting for the entire city watching him play for one team, then helicopter over to the next.

The Braves were headed back to the NLCS against last year's foe, the Pittsburgh Pirates. This series played out differently than the last. This time the Braves jumped out to a 3-1 series lead. It looked like another National League coronation. However, is anything ever THAT easy? Not here, for sure. The Pirates came storming back, and I mean all the way back. They tied the series at three games apiece and were sitting in the ninth inning of Game Seven with a 2-0 lead. Their starter Doug Drabek, who I always thought actually resembled a pirate, had shut the Braves down for the first eight innings. We were about to blow the series in typical Atlanta fashion. Not many teams in baseball history had ever blown a 3-1 series lead, especially with the final two games at home. But here we were, at the precipice of disaster. This seemed to be the Curse at its finest.

Then, perhaps the most exciting moment in Atlanta sports history occurred. At least, it was my favorite moment. Our hero Pendleton, again displaying a knack for the clutch, led off the inning with a double. After an error by Pirates second baseman Jose Lind and a walk, the Braves had bases loaded with no outs. Pirates closer Stan Belinda was summoned from the pen to secure the Pirates' historic series comeback. Outfielder Ron Gant stepped up to the plate and hit a ball like I had seen him hit many times. As my family sat around our little television set in our parents' bedroom, we all jumped, screamed and thought Gant had just hit a game-winning grand slam. It was not. Just a long sacrifice fly, but an out, nonetheless. After another walk and another out, our third string catcher, Francisco Cabrera, strode to the plate. Game Seven. Bases loaded. Ninth inning. Two outs. Down 2-1. Isn't this every kid's dream? Except, in my dream, it wasn't Francisco Cabrera. For some, that may have seemed like a nightmare. I'm pretty sure, had I laid money on him to be the player to come up with one of the most well-known hits in baseball history, I'd be a wealthy man. It was HIS moment, but it felt like ours as well.

Cabrera stroked a line drive that rolled into the glove of none other than Barry Bonds. One run came in for the tie, but Gold Glover Bonds would surely throw out the slowest-footed player on the Braves, Sid Bream. Miraculously, though, Bream beat the throw, the Braves won the game and Cabrera became part of baseball lore. Braves announcer Skip Caray's voice still rings in my ears,

"Braves win! Braves win! Braves win! Brave win! Braves win!!!!!!". It was such a sublime moment. This was certain to be the Braves year. There could be no doubt that destiny was now on our side. I know I had those thoughts. I'm pretty sure every Braves fan had those thoughts.

It was around this time we began to learn about a more sinister side of our beloved Curse. You see, as I've stated before, what makes this Curse more dastardly than others is the premature joy that always seems to accompany it. And there was no greater joy than watching tortoise-paced Sid Bream trucking it around the bases, sliding home to the greatest sports celebration I had ever seen. That was definitely the highest of the high moments. I could barely breathe when the excitement was all over (Sid Bream, at the bottom of the pile, probably couldn't either). My wife, Misty, loves to remind me (rub it in my face?) that she was, in fact, at that game. A truth that I am unabashedly jealous of. Of all the games, in all of the sports, I would have wished to have been at, that was it. As emotional as it was for my family in front of our television set, I can only imagine what it felt like to actually be there. It was THAT good.

Utter elation, only to be followed by bitter disappointment. That's what we have come to expect. This time, elation took the form of Francisco Cabrera, the last player on the bench, doing what no one expected. What form would the disappointment take on? As it turned out, the disappointment was an all too familiar face.

In the 1992 World Series against the Toronto Blue Jays, we were playing one of the truly most talented teams in recent memory. The Blue Jays lineup was full of all-stars up and down it. The Braves were good too, though. It was a pretty evenly-matched Series, but the Jays came up big just a couple more times late in games. The biggest moment, of course, occurred when Bobby Cox did the unthinkable, bringing in Charlie Leibrandt again. One of my favorite scenes in *The Lion King* was the moment leading up to Simba returning home to Pride Rock and become the King he was destined to be. In the scene, baboon and local shaman, Rafiki, wallops Simba over the head with his staff. After Simba questions the intention, Rafiki swings again. This time, however, Simba ducks, with the staff missing the mark. Simba, again a little puzzled, hears Rafiki sagely teach this lesson, "You can either run from the past, or you can learn from it." Wise words from a baboon. Unfortunately, Cox had a nasty habit of never learning from the mistakes of his past. An appropriately-placed baboon in the dugout sure would have been nice. Charlie Leibrandt "take-two" had turned out as bad as the first. Dave Winfield had his moment, as did the Blue Jays, and our elation had once again turned to disappointment.

Can a city keep coming back from such mental body blows? Well, we learned the answer to that question was a resounding YES. However, the body blows were just beginning. To use boxing lingo, we were witnessing a few jabs, perhaps a few shots at the ribs. The upper cuts and right hooks hadn't even begun yet, but the sense that we'd better start searching for our mouth guard was becoming increasingly evident.

The 1993 Braves season was yet another masterpiece. In what has been called by some "the last great pennant race", the Braves battled the San Francisco Giants in a can-you-top-this chase for the division. The Giants, for their part, raced out to a huge National League West lead on the backs of - guess who - newly acquired Barry Bonds. They were cruising through midsummer, until the Braves caught fire. Literally. On July 20, the press box at old Atlanta-Fulton County Stadium caught fire just a few hours after the Braves acquired all-star slugger Fred

McGriff in a trade. That night, the night of the fire, McGriff debuted with a late game-tying homerun that sparked the Braves towards a torrid finish. You can't write moments like this. They say truth is always better than fiction, but this was incredible. The Giants stayed hot, but in the end the Braves finished a measly, yet gigantic, one game ahead. On the last day of the season, the Dodgers beat the Giants, returning the favor from two seasons earlier.

For three months every game seemed to have something riding on it. It was as thrilling and nail-biting as they come, but the Braves were victorious. They were also easily favored in the playoffs over the try-hard Philadelphia Phillies. But as we know, it's never THAT easy. This series had blowout or sweep written all over it. Braves had players with titles such as MVP or Cy Young Winner all throughout. The Phillies had players with nicknames like "Nails" and "Wild Thing". You tell me who you would favor. Indeed, the Braves were better. In fact, they outscored the Phillies in the six-game series 33-23. Clearly the Braves were headed to another World Series. Right? Well, not exactly.

Somehow, the Phillies won a series in which they were completely out-manned and out-matched. The villain in my household was Phillies outfielder Pete Incaviglia, perhaps the worst defender in baseball history. No, he was absolutely the worst defender in baseball history. Except in this series. I'm telling you, I've never seen any player produce more game-changing diving catches than Incaviglia did in these six games. Considering the Braves lost THREE one-run games, every one of his plays was a difference maker. These were catches that he never, and I mean NEVER, would have usually made. But, in this series, he made every single one. I can't believe Incaviglia has not gone down in baseball legend for his acrobatics versus the Braves. My brothers and I had a new Curse whipping boy. His name was Pete Incaviglia, and he represented everything we were becoming all too familiar with. Without his out-of-body experience for the Phillies, the Braves most likely win the Series in no more than five games. At least, that's what we thought. But, keep in mind, the Curse will always find an Incaviglia somewhere down the line to do us in. Imagine losing a series in which you OUTSCORED your opponent by TEN runs. Unfortunately, we were getting used to this.

Unfortunately, I have said the word "unfortunately" way too often, and I will continue to do so out of sheer necessity. This series, again, demonstrates the nature of the Curse. We reach impossible levels of confidence, only to be slammed back down to earth. Somehow, it kept happening. And happening. And happening. And hap..

Can we take a breather here for a minute? I know exactly how all of this turned out and even I'm starting to get a little depressed. Atlanta was struggling to win, despite the multiple opportunities. The Falcons, Hawks, Braves, and Dawgs couldn't get over the top for anything. But the city did have a few successes; they just weren't the ones we all wanted. Evander "Real Deal" Holyfield, famously and proudly from Atlanta, became boxing's heavyweight champion, when that title actually mattered. He beat rival Mike Tyson twice, among others, despite infamously losing an ear in the process. That was a pretty cool moment for the city, but we are really grasping at straws if we are counting that as a win for the city. I was a Holyfield fan as much as the next, but I certainly wasn't sitting there saying the Curse has been broken.

The city even had a little football success, as the Georgia Tech Yellow Jackets shared the college football championship with Colorado. Even that, though, was tainted. Tech should have been outright champs, were it not for Colorado's "fifth down" game against Missouri and a phantom penalty against Notre Dame in the closing seconds of their bowl game. However, here's the thing. I'm sure the fifty or so Tech fans in the state of Georgia were thrilled. The rest of us took it as another dagger. As you may already know, Georgia Tech is UGA's long-time, hated rival and adversary. To the masses around these parts, there was little celebration, rather wistfulness, as to why couldn't that be us. Tech's title was nice, but 99.9% of the state was chomping at the bit for Georgia to be standing in the winner's circle again.

As for the Curse, for the majority of us, it lived on. The Falcons were still stumbling, the Hawks were very consistent (consistently average), and Georgia was never quite good enough to matter. The Braves WERE good enough to matter, but hadn't yet been the ones standing when the dust had settled. They were in contention for the World Series title every year, but were generally regarded as the Buffalo Bills of baseball. Get close, but never seal the deal. They epitomized "Loserville". However, that all changed in 1995.

Finally, this was the year when everything fell into place. The Braves won their division with ease, they swept the Cincinnati Reds right out of the League Championship Series, then out-classed the Indians in the World Series. Tom Glavine pitched the game of his life in the clincher (thank you Tommy) and David Justice put his money where his mouth was with a game-winning home run to finish off the Indians in Game Six (thank you David). We loved Justice for his boldness and brashness, calling out the fans to get their butts off their seats and cheer like maniacs. Sometimes, that's what it takes to win these kinds of things, not being "even-keeled", as Bobby Cox would tell you.

We actually had done it. We had climbed the mountain and could plant our flag. Even though an overriding emotion was relief, I'm not going to lie, it was very satisfying. I said to my dad a few minutes after the win, "I think I could live on this for years!" Shame on me for so frivolously uttering those words. I was a stupid 20-year-old kid. I didn't know what I was saying. Years? Really? I sure hope Tecumseh wasn't listening.

Although the victory was sweet (I must have watched the championship commemorative video something like a thousand times over the next year), I have now come to realize that the Braves win in 1995 was actually still the Curse doing his thing. Consider the following points of argument. First, as I said before, winning is great, but now that would be the only expectation. Anything less will not satisfy. Once you've reached the top, there's only one place to go. Now, even I am not fully convinced by that argument. I would take that sweetheart of a deal any day. But facts are facts: when you have won only a single championship in all those professional sports seasons, there is still something of a pit remaining in your stomach.

Secondly, Atlanta was actually gaining some momentum around the nation for its Curse. The name "Loserville" was beginning to catch on. We had an identity and, now, all of that was wiped away. Now, we were in no man's land. We weren't a historically great franchise (yet), nor were we anyone's "lovable losers". Even still, I think I'd rather have that chip to put on my mantle. Doesn't a student who typically makes poor grades still put his only "A" paper on the refrigerator? Of course they do. We were proud of this, as well we should have been. A few more like this would have also been nice. I know we had won only one title, but as a youngster I was greedy. I wanted a dynasty and I thought we had the team to do so.

Thinking back on that 1995 championship season, I had this striking thought. How could my accursed city actually be allowed to claim the ultimate prize? Did anyone notice the two participants in this series were the Braves and the Indians? Two teams with Native American mascots. How ironic that the Braves won it all that year, of all years. It is clear that Tecumseh sat this one out. That's the only explanation. But the thing is, if he was willing to give us this one moment of ultimate exhilaration, does that mean we were due a moment of ultimate sorrow in return? Did the Curse have something up its sleeve all along? Should we, as a city and fanbase, have expected some sort of retaliation for this one instance of glory? What possibly could the 1996 season have in store for us? Certainly, nothing that will occur could take away the immense joy we felt in our celebration. We even said that this win wipes away all that has happened before and all that will happen in the future, didn't we? Boy, were we wrong.

The Curse had taken a break for intermission, but Act II was getting ready to begin. The Curse was warming up its voice backstage, preparing for its showstopping reappearance. Unfortunately (there's that word again), the Curse had not yet reached the climax of this performance, and it was ready to step to the forefront and shine. As destiny directed Tecumseh to enter from stage left, we all sat with our hands folded in our laps not understanding what was about to happen. And then it did.

Chapter 7

The Turning Point

In 1996, all seemingly was right in the world. The Braves had won the title the previous year and now were firmly the team to beat. And no one could. They rolled through the regular season again, with an embarrassing riches of Cy Young Award winners. Just the names of Glavine, Maddux and Smoltz should have been enough to carry the Braves to the playoffs (and they were). Not only that, but newer names like Chipper and Andruw Jones, had joined the more familiar McGriff and Justice to form an intimidating offense. They had it all, including one of the most dominating closers in the game, Mark Wohlers. With another World Series win, Atlanta would have a dynasty on its hands and the Curse would become a thing of the past. All those years coming up short didn't seem so bad, now that we had the Braves. Be the first National League team to repeat as World Series Champs since the Big Red Machine of the 70's, and the Braves and our city would be immortalized. It was all right there to seize.

Atlanta coasted through the division and the first round division series against the Dodgers, but had to fight for their lives against the St. Louis Cardinals in the League Championship Series. Down 3 games to 1, the Braves turned to their three future Hall of Famers, the star-studded trio of Glavine, Maddux and Smoltz, to rescue them. And they did. Atlanta rallied for a 4-3 series win, cementing their spot in the World Series once again against the New

York Yankees. Again, we were experiencing the highest of highs. Unfortunately, we know what to expect after those moments of utter euphoria. Look out below!

The Yanks hadn't done too much over the last decade or so, and not much was expected of them here. The Braves were the clear favorites, and showed why for the first three and a half games. Notice, I said THREE AND A HALF games. Atlanta won the first two games with relative ease in New York. After giving the Yankees a game back in Game Three, the Braves took a 6-0 lead over the Yankees in Game Four. This game was another runaway, or so we all thought. The Curse was behind us now, only championships and parades awaited.

I was so ready to become one of those intolerable, snobby fans. Watching dynasties in other sports always had me salivating to be just like them. Those Celtics fans in basketball were insufferable. Those 49ers football fans were uppity and unbearable. I wanted that so badly. I wanted to snicker at fans of mediocre franchises behind their backs. Okay, that's a lie. I wanted to openly mock them, shame them for not being as good as we were. I wanted them to know we were a dynasty and they were not. Is that so wrong? After years of suffering at the hands of better, more fortunate teams, we were finally that team. Vanquish the Yankees and it would all be ours. Finish this series off and the Braves would be compared with the greatest teams of all time. This was going to happen in my city, for my team. That COULD HAVE been a beautiful thing.

It's those two little words, "could have", that kept all of this from happening. As in, the Braves could have been a dynasty. Or, the Braves could have been one of the greatest teams in baseball history. Or, worse, the Braves could have beaten those Yankees.

It sure looked like that was about to happen. After racing out to that six-run lead in Game Four, Atlanta slowly let New York back into game. However, we still led 6-3 into the seventh inning. That's when Bobby Cox brought in Mike Bielecki. Perhaps, outside of the baseball world, nobody remembers much about Bielecki. I sure do. Once a starting pitcher, his career was on the decline after injury. His ERA the previous season was an astoundingly high 5.97 for the California Angels. However, for this one magical season, Bielecki had reinvented himself as a reliever. Not only that, for this one season he seemed to possess a bionic arm. It's hard to imagine if you didn't live through it, but in 1996 he was almost untouchable. He was the bridge between our all-star starting pitchers and our all-star closer, Wohlers.

In the seventh inning, he came in against the Yankees. The plan seemed obvious. Bielecki would come in to pitch the seventh and eighth innings, as he had done before, then hand the ball off to Wohlers for the ninth. The first part of our strategy worked to perfection, as Bielecki cruised through the seventh. My brothers and I were high-fiving after that inning, and wanted more of Mike Bielecki. His arm was legend in our home. For some reason, his name never gets mentioned in Braves folklore, but in our house, he would always be remembered. Remembered, because he did not come back out for the eighth inning. Remembered, because instead of sticking with the plan, Bobby Cox decided to do something he hadn't done all season (sound familiar?). He brought in Mark Wohlers to pitch the final six outs, an expectation Wohlers was not accustomed to.

This was Cox, doing what Cox always did, overmanage, instead of sticking with the script. The Curse of Tecumseh must have loved Bobby Cox, making his job so much easier. The Curse probably invited Cox over to his house for Thanksgiving lunch and a little football. Or, perhaps, the Curse and Cox would go out for burgers every Saturday during the offseason. Who knows, maybe the Curse and Cox were both *Friends* fanatics, calling after every episode to discuss why Ross and Rachel were "on a break". For what it's worth, I was positive Bielecki would come back out for the eighth and was shocked when he didn't. It is historically understood that baseball players are creatures of habit, and get comfortable performing in their particular roles. Mark Wohlers was no different. This was a point of contention for us as we watched the game live, even before Wohlers threw his first pitch. Certainly, if novices like us had that thought, our Hall of Fame manager did, as well. You'd think so. But……..

After just ten pitches, Wohlers was already "in the soup", as they say. Two singles and an out had Jim Leyritz at bat with the count two balls and two strikes. Jim Leyritz. That name sends shudders right through my bones. This guy had no business doing anything special. I mean, seriously, have you ever seen that batting stance? Even Wohlers, not at his sharpest, should have handled Leyritz. However, he then threw that infamous slider. The slider that didn't really slide. The slider that sent shockwaves throughout the cosmos. The slider that could only be compared to things such as the sinking of Atlantis or the extinction of the dinosaurs. The slider that, if nothing else, changed the fortunes of two franchises forever.

Yes, Wohlers threw a slider. No, it was not a good one. Yes, Jim Leyritz crushed it to tie the game 6-6. No, the Braves did not regain momentum and win the game. When you put it like that, it sounds simple. In no way should this one instance in time ever be considered anything other than the most transformative instance in Atlanta sports history. Hanging a slider and getting it smoked happens daily in baseball, but this one was different.

Not only did the Braves blow a late six-run lead. Not only did they lose the second largest lead in World Series history. Not only did Cox make questionable call after questionable call, even after the Wohlers decision, that dearly cost the Braves in Game Four. They had handed the momentum to the Yankees on a silver platter. The Braves, the city and all of the fans were THIS close to having it all. One bad slider was all that was standing between us and immortality. The Yankees had stolen the momentum and the game. Jim Leyritz's name would now jump to the top of the list that already included Kent Hrbek, Scott Leius, and Pete Incaviglia, among others. But wait, you say, the series was still only two games apiece. The Yankees had not won the series. The Curse had not yet had the final say. We were the Braves, for goodness sakes, we were the next dynasty. Jim Leyritz wasn't going to take all of that away from us. Jim Leyritz couldn't single-handedly flip the entire universe on its head. Jim Leyritz couldn't possibly be destiny's chauffeur, with the Curse riding shotgun. Right?

In fact, the series was not over. Braves nation was staggering a little, but if last year had taught us anything, we knew we could win the grand prize. Game Five was our chance to take back control of the series and our fate. Win this game and all would be okay. Win this game and we are a single win away from dynasty. One win and Tecumseh can finally rest in peace.

It is interesting that history has stamped Game Four the turning point game. And, in reality, that game was a giant emotional roller coaster that gave the Yankees hope, where there almost was none. However, it was Game Five that was played with the series tied. Usually, those are considered the "turning point" games. And this one did not disappoint.

Atlanta's Smoltz and New York's Andy Pettitte were the game's starters. These two pitchers retired from baseball as the top two winners in postseason baseball history. Let's repeat that. This game featured a duel between the two pitchers who became the winningest postseason pitchers in the 100-plus years of the sport. How is this game not talked about more? World Series. Game Five. These two guys. What a treat. And neither one disappointed. Pettitte gave up no earned runs. Smoltz gave up no earned runs. Sounds like a draw. Except that it wasn't. Yes, Pettitte had a flawless line, but Smoltz was marred by the second most egregious play of the series and another in an increasingly long line of Curse moments.

Yankees outfielder Charlie Hayes hit a fly ball to Braves outfielder Marquis Grissom. Grissom was the four-time reigning Gold Glove center fielder. Yes, he was the best center fielder in the league. The only problem was, the ball was hit far enough to Grissom's left, that right fielder and rookie Jermaine Dye had also come towards the ball. It was Grissom's catch the whole way. However, Dye, inexplicably, cut right in front of Grissom just before the ball came down. Dye seemed to have shielded Grissom from clear sight of the ball, as the Braves' center fielder uncharacteristically dropped the ball. Grissom was, perhaps, the surest-handed glove in the game, but on this night, he simply missed the ball. Of all the nights and all the games and all the flyballs, this is the night that fate chose to tussle with Marquis Grissom. And when it comes to tussling with fate, fate always wins.

John Smoltz pitched another gem, but just like his 1991 Game Seven battle against Jack Morris, he was on the wrong side of a 1-0 loss. Imagine Smoltz for a minute. How snake-bitten must he have felt, having fallen AGAIN by a 1-0 score, this time on an error by his best defender. Smoltz was THIS close to having won two of the most thrilling and historic games in the history of the World Series. Yet, both times his team came up short. Both times his team could not muster even a single run. Both times he allowed no earned runs. Both times he was commended for his efforts, but not immortalized for his history-making performances. Baseball is a game of inches, but it always seems like destiny kept giving us that little extra nudge in the wrong direction. Had Jermaine dye crossed Grissom a split second earlier or later, the ball is easily caught, and the Braves might have won. Why do these nightmarish situations keep happening?

The Braves ended up losing, not only Game Five, but also Game Six and the Series. The Braves, who were just a few outs away from taking a commanding 3-1 series lead, lost it 4-2. Almost unimaginable. The crowning of the Braves as a dynasty would have to wait. As we will come to find out, 23 years later, we're still waiting. This series WAS the turning point for the Braves. Atlanta, on its way to becoming the team of the 90's and a team for the ages, was done. The Yankees, on the other hand, would go on to win 4 out of 5 World Series to steal the 90's and the ages away from the Braves. Jim Leyritz, he of the most ridiculous hitting posture the sport had ever seen, became the fulcrum on which destiny turned.

The Braves would still be a team to watch for the next umpteen years, but their shine was fading. After a series like that, you tend to reflect on how things might have been different. David Justice, one of our emotional leaders, was forced to miss the '96 Series due to injury. No doubt, that made a huge difference. Those kinds of things always do. We saw what Justice was capable of doing during the biggest of moments in the '95 series. As it turned out, Justice's absence forced Jermaine Dye into playing left field during that pivotal Game Five. Perhaps, had Justice been in the game instead of Dye, Grissom makes the catch and everything changes. We'll never know. The Curse never gave us the chance. Additionally, our talented reliever, Pedro Borbon Jr., was also injured before the Series with New York. I often have wondered if Cox would have put him in the game in that fateful eighth inning of Game Four, instead of Wohlers. This is the way things have always worked for our sports teams. When Borbon got injured, I hoped it would not come back to haunt us. It did. It always does. Imagine, the two pivotal plays in the series, the Leyritz homer and the Grissom error, were both aided by critical injuries that otherwise could have led to different outcomes. But, of course, they didn't play, and our hopes solely rested on Cox's playoff managerial prowess. We saw how that turned out.

In March of 1997, within a span of two days, all-stars Justice and Grissom were unnecessarily traded away, along with future all-star Jermaine Dye, and the makeup of the team was never the same. Had the Braves won the series, the trio of all-stars might still have been Braves and our fortunes may have been different. Fallout from the Curse had begun in earnest. For his part, Mark Wohlers was also never the same. He lost confidence in himself after the disastrous pitch to Leyritz. Within two years, Wohlers had actually lost the ability to even throw a strike. I mean at all. Pitches were either two feet above the catcher's glove or two feet in front of the plate. He literally could not get the ball to the catcher's glove and was gone by the 1999 season. That was the saddest part of what had resulted from this series. I was a huge Wohlers fan and it was hard for all of us to see what became of his career.

    The Curse had made a dramatic comeback. The sweet taste of victory in '95 had been replaced by the bitter pill of defeat. As a city, we were no longer reveling, but we were reeling. We were no longer celebrating; instead we were mourning. Mourning the loss of a championship that was in the palm of our hand. Mourning the loss of a rare opportunity for greatness. Mourning the loss of everything that we had built over the last five seasons. It was all gone. The 90's would now and forever belong to the Yankees.

The Curse had held sway over every mortal effort. As is its way, it gaveth and it tooketh away, once again. Once again, the euphoric high was replaced with a bottomless pit of despair. This time, however, the bottomless pit took a year to reveal itself. But, as I have said before, the higher the euphoria, the deeper the pit will be when the inevitable collapse occurs. After the win in '95, as a city and a sports community, we could not have been higher. But, somehow, none of that mattered anymore. It was almost as if it didn't happen, even though we all know it did. The Curse had struck once more. And it hammered with a vicious blow, with a force so violent that the ramifications are still being felt to this day. That World Series of 1996 was, in fact, the ultimate turning point for all that we could have become and all that we actually became.

Every loss hurts. However, no one can argue that some losses hurt much worse than others. Somehow, we have mastered losing when it seems impossible. Somehow, we have made disasters out of celebrations. Somehow, we always snatch defeat from the jaws of victory. Somehow, our moments of triumph are ALWAYS overtaken by subsequent moments of disillusionment and bewilderment. Why would we trust it will ever be different? Why do we always get drawn back in when the chance at history arises? Hadn't we finally learned our lesson after another debacle in 1996? In short, NO. As history will go on to show, we kept coming and kept coming back for more. In 1996, we were demoralized, but the worst, the absolute, most over-the-top worst, was yet to come.

There is one footnote to the 1996 Atlanta Braves season that must be added. We must spend a moment to give the Curse and its namesake, Tecumseh, a few props. How creatively despicable was it to have this absolute destruction of any "vestiges" of morale to be at the hands of the Yankees? As in Sherman's Yankees. Those old rivals from the North, who ravaged the city and state back in 1864. Their victory was, again, at our expense. The Yankees? Tecumseh may have taken 1995 off against the Indians, but came roaring back with a vengeance the next season in a most ironic twist. Can you believe it? At this point, yes. Absolutely. Nothing can be a surprise. Well done, Curse. Well done.

After 1996, nothing has been the same. Not for the Braves. Not for any of our other teams.

Chapter 8

Dark Side Of The Curse

The Braves dominated the Atlanta sports conversation for several years. Obviously, when your team is in the World Series FOUR times, you deserve all the attention. Winning only one time, however, left our city regretful of what might have been. Instead of rejoicing in becoming a team of destiny, we were remorseful for being broken by it. We were a team of almosts. We were a team of narrow misses. We were a team that always came up just shy. That was our identity. And it was hard to take. It was hard hearing how the national media viewed my team. It was hard seeing the narrative that had formed, and it seemed cemented in time. No longer was the upcoming season full of optimistic hope, rather it was filled with questions of how we might blow it this time. Invariably, we always did blow it. And then some.

We had graduated to Curse High School. We were no longer the wide-eyed newcomer. We had scars. Several of them. Those scars were fresh and still a little tender, but we couldn't understand at the time that those "scars" were merely flesh wounds. In the grand scheme of what was to happen over the next 20 years, we had only been poked and prodded. In time, we would be mercilessly and painfully branded by the Curse. Nevertheless, we were past the point of skepticism, and were beginning to understand that our fate might already be written in the stars. However, we weren't quite ready to confront the stark reality of our place in the sports galaxy. None of us were eager to look through the telescope of truth, but it was truth nonetheless and it would reveal itself in due season.

Losing baseball games, coming up short in slam dunk contests and continually drafting players that have no business suiting up is one thing. However, Atlanta was soon to see a much darker side to the Curse. A Curse that transcended sports. A Curse that affected our teams and city in a much different way.

In 1996 (before the Braves crashed and burned against the Yankees), Atlanta was the mecca of the sports world, in a way that made our little local teams appear insignificant. Our Atlanta had somehow been selected as host city for the '96 Summer Olympic Games. This was, without a doubt, the greatest coup in our city's history. How did a city of our pedigree earn the right to hold the largest sporting event in the world? As *Sesame Street* once asked, which of these is not like the other? MOSCOW. LOS ANGELES. SEOUL. BARCELONA. atlanta. SYDNEY. ATHENS. BEIJING. LONDON. RIO DE JANEIRO. TOKYO. Yes, that is a complete list of the cities to host the Summer Olympics from 1980 to the upcoming 2020. We looked like a little brother trying to compete against his much bigger and more talented older sibling. We just didn't quite seem to measure up. Still, there we were, with the world on our doorstep (our front porch probably wasn't nearly as grand as those other cities, though). Were we really going to pull this off? Surely, the Curse would leave us well enough alone, taking two weeks off to enjoy the Olympics himself. Surely, the stench of Atlanta's malodorous sports past would not spoil the Centennial Games. Wait. Did I hear *Centennial*? Yes. Not only did the International Olympic Committee deem our little town (comparatively little, mind you) appropriate to host the Games at all, they considered us worthy to showcase the 100th Anniversary Games. Are you kidding me? How did we not know this might not end well? Amazingly, Atlanta seemed to pull it off. We built venues left and right, reinvigorating the downtown area. It was definitely a city-wide effort. It seemed as though everyone was somehow involved. The opening ceremonies were a little hokey, but they were true to our city. Did you think the world was not going to be subjected to Alan Jackson's Chattahoochee at some point? I thought the pickup trucks and cheerleaders parading around in front of world leaders and diplomats was an especially nice touch. Y'all gotta love us.

In truth, other than miserable traffic flow, I thought the Games were outstanding. Perhaps, a little too commercial. Perhaps, a little too crowded. However, all in all, we were tremendously enjoying the show. I even got to see a USA vs. Cuba baseball game (of course, we lost, despite a late rally). All seemed well in our bubble. My family couldn't wait for Olympic Committee President Juan Antonio Samaranch to utter his famous line at the end of the Games. At all previous closing ceremonies he had presided over, Samaranch famously praised the city, calling the Games "the best ever". We didn't want the Olympics to end, but that was one thing we were greatly looking forward to. I couldn't wait for my city to be "the best ever".

However, on July 27 the unthinkable happened. At around 1:20 AM, the beautiful Centennial Olympic Park was the target of a bombing. All joking aside, this was a heinous act and a somber moment, not only for our city, but for the world. The Olympics are seen as a symbol of unity throughout, in spite of what may be happening in the political arena. Two weeks where countries of all races and creeds could compete, demonstrating sportsmanship and virtue. This was a cold reminder of the world around us, encroaching on our innocence. This time, evil and hate had taken center stage, with the bomb killing two and injuring 111. It was, however, wonderful to see countries come together and condemn such a wretched act. Unfortunately, the damage had been done.

In the end, it was impossible, even for us, not to associate the '96 Olympics with the bombing. In the end, our Games were forever marred by this atrocity. And, in the end, Juan Antonio Samaranch did not call the Olympics "the best ever". For me, that was a real kick in the gut. Please forgive me if I still harbor a little ill-will towards the IOC President. Atlanta had done its best. We were not to blame for the Park Bombing. Yet, even Samaranch himself, lumped us in together, when he called our Games "most exceptional". In truth, perhaps, Samaranch was right in his statement. How could these possibly have been the "best" Games ever, when such an event had occurred?

Off the field incidents were rather commonplace for our city. Many times it wasn't a pretty look. Case in point, was Super Bowl XXXIII (that's 33, for all you non-Romans) on January 31, 1999. Believe it or not, our beloved Atlanta Falcons finally had their magical season. The original "Dirty Birds" themselves, as they were known, had an incredible 14-2 season. There were few legendary names on that team, except maybe kicker Morten Andersen. You know you don't have a lot of star power when your most well-known player is your Danish kicker. But here we were, everything had gone our way. Our team of no-names was on the edge of history. I know, I know, we've seen this before. This time, though, sure looked different.

In the NFC Championship Game, just a stone's throw from reaching the ultimate game, we faced off against the Minnesota Vikings, who were actually the favored team. The Vikings that season went a preposterous 15-1, with one of the most dynamic offenses in history. All-Pro players read up and down their roster, including Randall Cunningham, Randy Moss, Chris Carter, John Randle, and kicker Gary Anderson (don't forget that name).

From the start, it appeared Minnesota had the upper hand. Playing in front of their home crowd in the Metrodome seemed to give them an advantage, as well. We all remembered the Metrodome, that most hated stadium, from the 1991 World Series against the Twins. Was it again to be a house of horrors for our team? It sure looked like it early on, as the Vikings led 20-7 late in the first half, a lead that could have been worse had Moss not dropped a sure touchdown pass. A lead that appeared to be growing, as the Vikings were on the drive again with the second quarter winding down. However, our playmaker, defensive lineman Chuck Smith, sacked quarterback Cunningham, causing a fumble recovered by the Falcons. We scored just before the half to keep it a manageable game.

Through it all, the Vikings were convincingly in control, but couldn't put the Falcons away. Every time they were about to drive the stake through Atlanta's heart, Minnesota would throw us a life preserver of hope. However, with just over two minutes remaining the Vikings had the final stake in hand. The Falcons were firmly planted in their coffin of defeat, with Minnesota ready to nail it shut. And the last rites were about to be read by Vikings kicker Gary Anderson.

Curse deny-ers will say that our sports teams have won some pretty big games. They say, how can we claim a curse, when we have seen several monumental victories (perhaps, Francisco Cabrera in 1992 comes to mind). However, keep in mind what has followed almost each and every one of those moments of exhilaration and triumph. What's about to happen in this game will be just another notch on Tecumseh's belt. What we are about to witness will result in just another plaque for the Curse trophy case.

Gary Anderson was the butt of many a joke within my family. He was very likely the last NFL player to wear just a single-barred face mask. Just this fact alone made him fodder for our mockery. He wasn't even pretending as though he would ever "mix it up" on the field. A single-barred face mask. Really? You just wanted to see a big, ugly lineman rub his face in the dirt a little. Just once. He sure seemed to be asking for it. However, this season, nobody was making fun of Anderson. He had become the first kicker in the HISTORY of the sport to not miss a single kick. Get this straight, he made EVERY kick he took during the season and in the playoffs, up to this point. He was a machine. A machine that was lining up to take a chip-shot field goal, one that would have certainly sealed the win for the Vikings and sent them to the Super Bowl. As automatic as any kicker had ever been.

If there was ever a moment a team had the right to start measuring their fingers for championship jewelry, that was it. It was a paltry 39 yards. It was indoors, so there was no wind, except the collective exhale from Viking fans knowing they were about to win. Anderson could make a 39-yard kick blindfolded. Probably blindfolded, with both hands tied behind his back. He could have made it with his other foot. He could have made that kick in his sleep. Except, he didn't.

For the first time all season, in the moment that mattered the most, he missed. How? What force could have caused this aberration? His name is Tecumseh and he gently nudged that short field goal just outside the goal post. Why would the Curse HELP us, you say? Have you not been reading this far? The Curse didn't want us to just lose, he wanted us to be crushed. He wanted us to start handing out championship t-shirts. He wanted us to get the celebration champagne on ice inside our locker room of hope.

Anderson did miss. And the Falcons drove down the field to tie the score at 27 with overtime looming. Of course they did. The Vikings nearly intercepted a pass during that tying touchdown drive, but incredibly missed that opportunity as well. Karma had come calling in Minnesota and it wasn't kind to the Vikings. They were to become debris left on the side of the road by the force of our Curse. In overtime, Falcons' kicker Morten Andersen, solidified his spot in Atlanta lore by making an eerily similar 38-yard kick to send the Dirty Birds wing-flapping all the way to the Super Bowl. In the battle of Andersons (Andersens?), ours had won. Our Danish-born Andersen had done what Minnesota's South African-born Anderson could not. Kickers in the NFL live such a tenuous existence. The difference between hero and fall guy is so miniscule. Could it all have possibly come down to simple name spelling? Do the sports gods favor Danish kickers? Could it solely have been a result of the number of bars on the face mask? Who knows? Poor Gary Anderson, and his lone missed kick of the season, walked off the field that day, watching the Falcons celebrate in his own stadium.

Definitely, a fortunate moment for our (usually) unfortunate city. Can you believe it? The Falcons were going to the Super Bowl, facing the defending champion Denver Broncos, with a chance to win it all. Win this game, the biggest of all games, and you will never be forgotten. Win one more game and Atlanta has a Super Bowl trophy to call its own. The whole world will be watching. As big as the World Series was, this was bigger. This is the head honcho of championship games. This was the Big Kahuna. This was the Grand Poobah. This was..

This was just another opportunity for the Curse to give us the falsest of hopes. We've been down this road before and it appears more like a dark alley. Could this time be different? Foolish thoughts. However, for some strange reason the Falcons had a believer. I completely had bought into the hype. The way we had beaten the Vikings said it all. We were the team of destiny this year. Everything that needed to go right, went right. It was FINALLY our time. We all just knew it. YEAH, RIGHT. Cue Eugene Robinson. Cue Miami night life. And, once again, cue the Curse.

Every year the NFL hands out the Bart Starr Award, annually given out to the player who "best exemplifies outstanding character and leadership in the home, on the field, and in the community". In 1998, that award went to the Falcons safety Eugene Robinson. Robinson was considered the spiritual leader of the Falcons. He was their veteran presence and beacon of light. If there was one player the Falcons knew they could count on, it was Eugene Robinson. Except, this time they couldn't.

Player rituals the night before the biggest game of their lives are an individual thing. I'm sure every player does something different. Some want to get a good night's rest to be in optimal form the next day. Some can't sleep and they spend the night visualizing what it will actually be like on that incredible stage. Some watch film and get technically prepared for the game. There's no end to what players may do to get their mind ready for the game of all games.

Eugene Robinson, the NFL's Bart Starr Award winner, prepared for the big day by soliciting a prostitute. That's right. The exact day Robinson was given the award for character and integrity, he was arrested in Miami on the eve of the Super Bowl. This may be a quality time to add another to our "only in Atlanta" list. As in, only in Atlanta can the NFL award recipient for character and leadership be arrested on the night before the Super Bowl.

Could you imagine Falcons coach Dan Reeves waking up to THAT? I wouldn't have wanted to be one of the underlings that broke the news to Reeves. In no way, could the coach have prepared for that moment, nor could have any of his players. Imagine the chatter around the breakfast table. No, it wasn't about game tactics. It wasn't about the excitement, or the opportunity, or what lie ahead later that day against John Elway's Broncos. It wasn't about a magical season that had seen the Falcons defy their woeful past in extraordinary fashion. No, it was about Eugene Robinson, their voice and their leader, stamping his fingerprints and posing for his mug shot only hours earlier. All the preparation that had led to this instance meant absolutely nothing. Instead of being loose for the upcoming extravaganza, Atlanta was inextricably tense. You can tell yourself you wouldn't be affected by such a circumstance, but how could you not? Of all the issues Coach Reeves considered having to handle, this certainly was at the very bottom of the list. This was more than a brief distraction. It was more than a mild disturbance. This was a game-changer.

Let's not pretend like the Falcons were heavy favorites in this game. They weren't. And the Broncos needed no added advantages. Yet, we gave them one. A big one. And they DID take advantage. Once the game began, though, my thoughts were no longer on Robinson. All I could think about was our chance to hang a banner. Our opportunity to hoist the ever-iconic Lombardi Trophy. One win and it was ours. Eugene Robinson's indiscretion would be a thing of the past, if we could just win this one little game. No longer were we focused on Robinson and his ill-timed lapse of judgement. But you know who was? Eugene Robinson.

As if on cue, the biggest play of the game involved none other than, you guessed it, Eugene Robinson. Should we not have expected this to be the case? What in Atlanta sports history would lead you to believe that Robinson's failings would not be significant. For us, in Atlanta, the chickens always come home to roost. On this night, the chicken not only roosted, it laid a couple of eggs along the way.

All quarterback John Elway needed was a split second to take advantage of our preoccupied defensive back Robinson. With the outcome of the game still in doubt, Elway roasted him for a back-breaking 80-yard touchdown pass to Rod Smith, a play that saw Smith flashing past the indecisive Robinson. This play turned the game into a rout, and the Falcons never recovered. Of course they didn't. Was Robinson's mind, perhaps, on something else? Could he have been overly aggressive, in an attempt to redeem himself? Was he simply not sharp, having spent the previous night involved in everything EXCEPT game preparation? Surely, the events of Super Bowl Eve had impacted his performance. How could they not? I can still envision Robinson chasing Smith down the field in futility, attempting to salvage something, anything. What do you think was going through his mind in that flash of a moment? One could only guess. I'm sure, at some point, he wished the Vikings' Anderson had actually made the kick, wiping all of this from memory. But it wasn't to be.

This game got ugly early and often. After the demoralizing Robinson play, the Broncos jumped out to a 31-6 fourth quarter lead and the game was essentially over.

The Falcons, just like that, had found themselves losing by 25. Anyone watching that game knew it was over. It is mortally impossible to overcome a 25-point Super Bowl deficit. It didn't matter if the score was 31-6 or 45-20 or **28-3**, TWENTY FIVE points is TWENTY FIVE points. Never, as long as time itself exists, will a team win a game after trailing by such a margin. Not the Falcons. Not anybody else. WILL NEVER HAPPEN!!! Does the phrase "when pigs fly" have any meaning? As in, a team will overcome a 25-point Super Bowl deficit when pigs fly. Well………………………………

Okay, enough foreshadowing already. In this game, the Falcons did not come back. They lost the Super Bowl to a team that was far superior on this night. Was it because of Eugene Robinson? We'll never really know. Except, like we've said before, there always does seem to be a Eugene Robinson. And, as far as I can tell, there always will.

Once again, we were Curse-bitten. The miraculous comeback against the Vikings was a distant memory. Once again, we were found looking through the store window, desiring what we will never be able to afford. Again, it happened. It always happens. And it likely always will.

Chapter 9

The Good, The Bad and the Ugly

If I'm being truthful, this chapter should probably be titled *The Bad, the Ugly and the Utterly Ridiculous,* as there was very little good. With the Super Bowl disaster behind us, we looked to the future and wondered, "What next?". Sometimes, it's difficult coming to grips with who you are. Nobody wants to examine their own warts. And we had a lot of warts. The problem was that few outside of Atlanta noticed. For some reason, that made it seem a lot worse. Over the years, I've wanted to jerk the television from the wall every time I watched ESPN talk about fan apathy at the games. Talking heads would routinely and increasingly disparage Atlantans for empty stadium seats. It became chic to criticize our fans for lack of support. Are you kidding me? After years of "close, but no cigar," it became an all-too-arduous task for many fans to stay invested. The pundits would say things like, "If they were better sports fans, this stadium would be packed." That generalization was never fair to all of us amazing and deep-rooted fans.

However, there is no doubt it became increasingly more and more difficult to stay rabid. Instead of going to games with the grandest of dreams, you chose to stay cloistered in your house, watching in sickening silence.

You would go from enjoying the game with friends, to wanting to watch privately and suffer alone. Instead of keeping your eyes glued to every second of action, unable to turn away, you've now become someone that has to walk out of the room every time a big moment occurs. It all just becomes much too grueling. I will admit it, as a sports fan, I have changed. I didn't used to be this way. The Curse has definitely changed me. Try living through the years we have endured, then tell me if you'd spend your money, time, investment or emotions to watch something like Game Five of the 1997 National League Championship Series against the Florida Marlins.

The 1997 baseball season again saw the Braves run away with the best record in the National League. The nearest team was the Marlins, NINE games behind us in our own division. Florida had some good players; mostly veterans poached from other teams, but in no way should they have been competitive with the Braves. To me, the weight of losing the '96 Series to the Yankees (as well as all of the others) was still hanging over Atlanta. As a fan, you are eternally hopeful, but it just wasn't the same as in 1991 or 1992. You've seen how this plays out one too many times. But that ONE championship back in 1995 at least gave us some shred of hope.

Actually, winning the World Series in '95 has been the chief reason we keep getting emotionally dragged back in. We always tell ourselves, "Well it happened once, it can happen again." Is there any doubt now, in light of the mounting evidence, that the Curse only *appeared* to turn the other cheek in 1995? Is there some chance this was all part of Tecumseh's plan? The one title given, though more of a noose, was only used to rope us in every year. What's the fun in a curse if nobody cares? It was diabolical, really. We cared, yet we knew we would ultimately lose. Still, we kept coming back year after year, season after season, because of that tiniest of faint hope that '95 had given us. Pure misery.

As the 1997 playoffs began, there we were again, the team to beat. The phrase, "the team to beat," sadly, has all new meaning to me now. It used to mean "the best" or "the standard," but now it feels almost like an inevitable death sentence. I imagined the Braves as an inmate on death row, awaiting the executioner. In 1997, the executioner was umpire Eric Gregg. After defeating the Houston Astros in the first round of the playoffs, we faced off against our division foe Marlins, a team that we had soundly beaten during the year. However, as seemed to be the case every year, our fate was out of our control.

With the series tied at two games apiece, crucial Game Five was played in Miami, and the home plate umpire was Eric Gregg. As they say, you know a good umpire, when you don't even notice them. Eric Gregg was the type that made sure he would never go unnoticed. As Game Five's typically go, this was the key turning point of the series. We had 4-time Cy Young Award winner Greg Maddux pitching. They had 22-year old Livan Hernandez, he of 17 total career starts, taking the mound. Let's get this straight, Greg Maddux, on the short list of greatest pitchers of all time, vs. Livan Hernandez, rookie and postseason neophyte. Despite all we had seen over the last few years, we were rightfully confident going into this game. Weren't we so cute back then? If this same situation were to arise now, I would almost guarantee us a loss. It happens every time. Jaded? You bet.

Let's just get this out of the way. The Braves lost the game 2-1. Clearly, Hernandez outdueled Maddux and pitched the game of his very young life. It can happen. We saw it in 1991 and 1992 with the young gun Braves. His stat line sure looked like he had a game like none other: 9

innings pitched, only 1 run and 3 hits allowed, to go along with 15 strikeouts on 143 pitches. Wow, what a night. What can you say? He was just better than us in this biggest of moments. Or was he?

First of all, how does it seem like EVERY SINGLE turning point moment turns for the opponent, never for us? Why do we never have the ultimate unsung hero that puts us over the top for good? Why do we always have to go down at the hands of a Scoot Leius, a Pete Incaviglia, a Jim Leyritz or, now, a Livan Hernandez? Although, here's the thing – Hernandez was good, but not THAT good. He had a little help. There's a reason why in Braves Country this has come to be known as the Eric Gregg Game. Not the Livan Hernandez Game. In hindsight, it is absurd how this game not only turned the series in the Marlins favor, it also took the Curse from the ridiculous to the sublime.

This is one of those times in life where you really had to be there to believe it. Livan Hernandez was throwing strike after strike, mowing the Braves down hitter after hitter. But therein lies the problem; he actually was NOT throwing strike after strike. Home plate ump Gregg was also having the game of his life. However, it was his absolute worst game. I never was a fan of Eric Gregg, but this was entirely too much. As most pitchers tend to do early in the game, you test the umpire's strike zone. Hernandez was no different on this night. Hernandez and catcher Charles Johnson obviously noticed early that Gregg was giving them a generous strike zone. As is customary, you take what you can get.

The Marlins battery mates, however, got quite a lot more than anyone could ever deserve. It seemed like each successive pitch was just a little bit more outside of the strike zone than the last. I'm telling you, if you didn't see this game, go back and watch the footage. Gregg was calling pitches that were two feet outside as strikes. TWO FEET. If you think I'm being in any way hyperbolic, just do an internet search for "Eric Gregg Braves Marlins" and see what comes up. I promise, you won't believe your eyes. My brothers and I, again watching this game together, couldn't believe our eyes. Was Eric Gregg a secret Florida Marlins fan? Was he being paid off to call every pitch a strike for Hernandez? Did he mistakenly think the plate was four feet wide, or leave his glasses in the hotel room? Any and all of these thoughts ran through my mind. As the game went on, things got increasingly more and more absurd. Pitches were called strikes that were so far outside to lefties, they would have hit a righthanded batter. I'm telling you, watch the tape. Seemingly pitch after pitch was further out than the last. Every time Gregg would "punch out" a batter, it was almost as if he was relishing the moment.

One of my favorite scenes in any movie is from *Naked Gun*. In this scene, actor Leslie Neilson plays opera-singer-turned-umpire Enrico Pallazzo. An undercover detective by trade, he finds himself behind the plate of a major league baseball game. In one of the funniest scenes from the movie, "Pallazzo" gets carried away with himself calling strikes as the home plate umpire. The first time he hears the crowd roar on a strike call, he is somewhat taken with the approval of the fans. As he begins to realize his power over fan reaction, he starts calling strikes with more and more gusto. By then end of the scene, with the crowd roaring at every strike call, he starts break dancing, as he sends batters back to the dugout.

Perhaps, I'm being a little unfair to Gregg (trust me, I'm not), but this was eerily similar. It seemed as though Gregg was pandering to the crowd in Miami. His strike calls became more demonstrative as the game wore on. As a Braves fan, we all saw it. He was reveling in the moment.

All eyes were on him and he loved it. He was unashamedly soaking up each and every ounce of fan adulation. It all culminated with the last batter for the Braves, Fred McGriff. With two outs and two strikes on McGriff, there had never been a more obvious next pitch. We knew it was coming. Certainly, Hernandez knew it was coming. Every fan in the stadium was expecting it. And even though Fred McGriff knew it was coming, there was nothing he could do about it. This was the moment, where all our emotions turned from disbelief to downright incredulity. Cue Livan Hernandez. Cue Eric Gregg. And cue the Curse.

The pitch left Hernandez's hand with only one intention - be as far off the plate as possible. And it was. The pitch was so ridiculously high and outside, I honestly don't believe McGriff could have even reached it. Hernandez knew it was a ball. McGriff knew it was a ball. All 51,982 fans in attendance knew it was ball. The millions at home knew it was a ball. However, the one that counted the most, did not. The one that had the fates of both teams and fan bases in his hands, "saw it differently". The one that was relishing every cheer from the Marlins' fans, called this most outlandish pitch strike three. The fans exploded, Gregg walked off the field congratulating himself, and the Braves had lost Game Five and eventually the series. McGriff didn't even argue the call. Why would he? It wouldn't matter.

My brothers and I have this hilarious re-enactment routine that we do at social events, especially among Braves loyalists. I pretend to be Livan Hernandez. My older brother, Danny, is the catcher. And my younger brother, and Enrico Pallazzo wanna-be, Tim, plays the role of Eric Gregg (to perfection, I might add). First, I pretend to "pitch" a ball just off the plate that Tim (Gregg) enthusiastically calls a strike. For my second pitch, Danny slides several feet outside, and when the next pitch is caught, Tim dances around the room calling strike two. On my third pitch, I wind up and *before the ball even leaves my hand,* Tim is prancing around the room, moonwalking a strike three call. We are certainly pandering to OUR audience of family and friends, much in the way Gregg seemed to do in that ludicrous Game Five. However, the reason our act is so wonderfully entertaining is because it is so accurate. Eric Gregg's name will continue to live on in infamy for us and for anyone rooting for the Braves who saw that game. What we witnessed in Game Five proved, once and for all, that truth is certainly stranger than fiction.

For the Braves, 1998 was the same story. Tell me if this sounds familiar. Atlanta absolutely destroys the National League once again, this time winning 106 games. Yeah, yeah, yeah, I know. Team to beat. Maddux, Glavine, Smoltz. Yada, yada, yada. Somehow, the Braves had made winning that many games mundane. Mundane because it was not only the same regular season script every year, but the same playoff script, as well. Rampage through the National League. Check. Get everybody's hopes way up. Check. Let us all down with a disappointing and dissatisfying playoff exit. CHECK. 1998 was no different. It seemed like each successive postseason, the Braves became a little more adverse to winning. Each year they seemed to put up less and less of a fight. And so it was against the San Diego Padres in the NLCS. Atlanta was eight games clear of San Diego during the season, but in this series, they almost looked overmatched.

Case in point were the two games started by Padre pitcher Sterling Hitchcock. The lefthander had a lifetime 74-76 record, certainly not the stuff of legends. However, in this series, against the Braves, he was almost unhittable. In two starts, Hitchcock gave up only 5 hits and a single run combined, stifling one of league's most powerful lineups. The Braves were outplayed and out-managed.

Padre manager Bruce Bochy, like so many before him, made all the right moves. While Braves manager Cox seemed to make one false step after another. Once again, Atlanta limped away without so much as a whimper.

It was sad to see. Even though the Braves were winning the National League East every year, the regression was obvious. Although, it probably wasn't as much regression as it was the weight of so many previous failures. In other words, they wilted under the weight of the Curse. Every time the stakes rose, the Braves crumbled. It seemed bad then, but as time will tell, it only would get worse. Much worse.

In 1999, the Braves………Stop me. Please. I can't take much more. Okay, let's get through this quickly. 103 wins. Chipper Jones, MVP. Team to beat. Hopes raised. Hopes crushed. Yep, that about sums it up. Honestly, it is a broken record. We all felt it then and, in retrospect, it looks even worse. How did any of us mentally survive? I mean, this whole thing is absolutely brutal. Each season seemed to grow longer and longer, wading through all of the regular wins and utter dominance, simply to get to an end-of-year collapse. At the start of each year, the feeling really wasn't of optimism, but more of "Can we get this over with already?"

Sure, Chipper was amazing. Pitching was amazing. And this time we actually were able to make it back to the World Series. Even though we had come to realize the only real certainty seemed to be an eventual Braves collapse, the Braves did, in fact, make it to the Show. And to make things a little more dramatic, we were facing the Yankees again. The national media made this series out as the battle for the team of the 90's. Yet again, I bought back into the hype. Yet again, shame on me. However, even though it had been three years, I still wanted revenge for that 1996

World Series. Maybe this was the year the Braves found redemption for themselves, for the fans and for all of Atlanta's sports. I actually thought that perhaps it was better that we had lost in '97 and '98 to less talented teams, only to have atonement against the team that had hurt us most. Maybe, the last few years had served a purpose. Maybe, everything had always been funneling us to this moment. Maybe, this was going to be the greatest comeuppance of all. It all sounded so good, if not meant to be.

      What happened was definitely meant to be. The Yankees demolished the Braves in a 4-0 sweep, running their World Series winning streak to an unreal 12 games (eight of those against our Braves). Not only was the outcome meant to be, it was inescapable. Haven't I seen enough? How many times am I going to get reeled back in? I shouldn't even care anymore. But I do. I wish my heart wasn't in my throat every time the Braves invariably botch another opportunity. But it is. I wish I could leave my sports fandom behind me and find another pastime. But I can't. I'm all in and it stinks.

Chapter 10

What Might Have Been...

    The 1990's were gone, and with it went the Atlanta Braves' World Series hopes. A ten-year run, like nothing our town had seen, was over. At the end of it all, we were only left with a giant lump of discouragement in our hearts. Those teams had five Hall of Famers, as well as several that are at least borderline. And yet, we could only muster that one championship. Would the Yankees of Ruth or DiMaggio or Yogi or Mantle have been happy to hoist the World Series trophy just once? Would the Lakers of Magic and Kareem or Shaq and Kobe have been satisfied with one title? Would the Cowboys of Aikman, Smith and Irvin have been considered a success had they won just a single Super Bowl? I'm guessing the answer to all of those is a resounding NO.

    When a franchise is blessed to have such an abundance of talent that remained together for a decade, you do and should expect more. Anything less than a dynasty is construed as a massive disappointment. And that is exactly how we all felt. Who was to blame? Was it Bobby Cox, who seemed to be regularly outmaneuvered by other managers come playoff time? Was it our all-star players, who so often came up small in the biggest moments? Was it simple dumb luck that gave us a decade's worth of unfortunate incidents? Whatever it was, it happened, and now it was over. As if to rub it in a little more, the 90's ended with Braves closer John Rocker getting suspended for the first month of the following season for comments he made in a *Sports Illustrated* article. In it, Rocker proceeded to offend every segment of the metropolitan New York population and beyond. After all the good the Braves had done, this would be the capstone memory. Sounds about right.

As we turned the page on the millennium, something magical seemed to happen in Atlanta sports. The Atlanta Falcons traded with the San Diego Chargers to acquire the first pick in the 2001 draft. And with that pick the Falcons selected Michael Vick. Who was Michael Vick? Only the most exciting player to grace a football field since, well....... since Deion Sanders. Michael Vick, the player that was destined to turn around the misfortunes of our entire city. The Falcons gave up 3 picks and a player for the rights to draft Vick, and from our vantage point then, it was absolutely worth it. How often do you get the chance at such a generational talent?

Vick burst on the scene in his second season in the league, after little playing time his rookie season. One particular moment sticks out to me from that 2002 season above all others. On December 1, the Falcons were playing the Minnesota Vikings (again), in a season that saw a resurgent Atlanta team vying for the playoffs. Keep in mind, this was Vick's first full season and the Falcons were already flying high. As in the 1999 playoffs, we again found ourselves in an overtime thriller with the Vikings.

Let's set the scene. With thirteen minutes remaining in overtime, Falcons are facing second down and 8 yards to go from the Viking 46-yard line. Then it happened. The next play will forever be etched in my mind. Snap. Vick rolls left. Magic happens. As quick as the blink of an eye, Michael Vick went from our future to our present. We went from the franchise nobody cared about to the one opening *SportsCenter*. Or, perhaps, as my brother Danny put it best later that day - we finally had THE player in an entire sport. We had Michael Jordan. We had Tiger Woods. Finally, Atlanta had the player everybody wanted to watch. Michael Vick was must-see television and he was all ours.

Oh yeah, and on that play, Vick raced down the field in a blur. As he raced towards the end zone, he split two Vikings players. He split them like a Ginsu knife, sharp and clean. The two defenders missed Vick entirely, colliding into each other, shredded by the swiftest blade of them all. The soon-to-be superstar ran it in for the game-winning touchdown. The image was so memorable. How did he slip through untouched? Was his second gear that much faster than everyone else's? The play said it all. Our best was better than yours, better than anyone else's. In our minds, San Diego had made the mistake of a lifetime, giving up the chance for a once-in-a-lifetime player like Vick. His final stat line in the game was noteworthy - 173 yards passing and 173 yards rushing. This was a player that was primed and ready to take our city to heights never before reached.

It turned out, the Falcons did reach the playoffs that year. Not only that, in the first round they traveled up north to Green Bay to face a Packers team led by All-Pro quarterback Brett Favre. Remember him? Over a decade later, here we were. Favre, now an MVP and a Super Bowl champion, reminding us of what we could have been. The star we gave away for a bag of balls versus the new face of the NFL. This was no easy task for the Falcons. Not only were we playing the likes of Favre, we were going up against history. A history that said we were playing a franchise that had never lost a home playoff game at Lambeau Field. Never. Think about the Packers and their playoff lineage. In all those years, not once had they come up short in their stadium. Not a single time. Until now. Michael Vick and his Falcons did the unthinkable. They actually beat Green Bay, on the road, with this magnetic athlete who had the whole town going gaga.

We didn't make it past the next round, however, against the more seasoned Philadelphia Eagles. We didn't care, the future was extraordinarily bright. It felt nice having that new car smell. The stench of being the favorite and losing (Braves) had grown tiresome. Losing when there are no expectations, as we have seen, simply doesn't hurt as much. The Falcons had a player that was going to lead our franchise to glory for the next fifteen years.

Two years later the Falcons made the playoffs again. This time we were not the upstarts. This time we had a first round bye. If you didn't know, having a first round bye is slang for "we have a team that can legitimately compete for a Super Bowl." In the divisional round we looked the part, demolishing the St. Louis Rams 47-17. Atlanta wasn't a newbie anymore. The Dirty Birds were back, baby. Back in the NFC Championship game for the first time in five years. Actually, considering the Falcons had played in exactly 0 NFC title games for their first 32 years of existence, playing twice in five years seemed like we had won the lottery. But these weren't your daddy's Falcons. We had expectations now. We had the most exciting player in the league now.

Unfortunately, this was also Atlanta, and lest we forget a little thing called the Curse. Atlanta's fate always seemed to twist and turn in only the most excruciating ways. Why should this be any different? The Falcons had just tossed the Rams aside with the greatest of ease. However, we were now at a point in time we had been MANY times. Our burgeoning hopes could end up one of two ways. We could either "rise up" …..or we crumble like a lying defendant in Judge Judy's courtroom. Let's just say, our eyes got a little shifty and our palms started sweating. We had been caught in the biggest lie of all, the one that said we could actually overcome Tecumseh.

In the NFC Championship game we again were facing the Eagles, the team that treated us like second-class citizens just two years earlier. This time, though, we weren't fresh-faced newcomers. This time we weren't party crashers, we were among the A-list invites. This time we were going to give Philadelphia a taste of their own medicine. This time, however, was no different. Once again, we were thoroughly dominated by the Eagles. Once again, Vick couldn't get us over the top. Once again, Atlanta had a franchise that couldn't get out of its own way and defy the long history of an ever-growing list of sports failures.

The Michael Vick-led Falcons limped away from Philadelphia, never to return to that spotlight again. In 2005, the Falcons went 8-8 and in 2006, they were 7-9. Amazingly, the futility of the Falcons franchise reached an ignominious mark of FORTY years without back-to-back winning seasons. Can you believe, not in forty years could a team finish even 9-7 twice in a row. Futility is not the right word for that; it is an absolute disgrace. However, we had not seen disgrace at its lowest just yet.

Michael Vick had only been in Atlanta six seasons, but the sense was growing that he was not going to lead our franchise to the promised land. Had this shooting star already lost his shine? Had we already seen the peak of the Michael Vick era? Perhaps he had little to no help, but it was hard to dismiss two consecutive non-winning seasons from the player we were anticipating leading us to prominence and prestige. But it wasn't just the losing. Vick began making headlines off the field, as well. And not for the reasons an Atlanta fan would want. The indiscretions grew worse and worse, and in just a few short months everything would be dramatically altered.

In November of 2006, Vick was fined by the league for making an obscene gesture at a heckling fan. *Strike One.* Just two months later, Vick had a water bottle confiscated by airport security, when a secret compartment contained what appeared to be indications of an illegal substance. Officials, however, dropped all charges due to insufficient evidence. That's like eating the last cookie out of the cookie jar, but there are no crumbs left as evidence to identify you as the culprit. *Strike Two.* Not only were we no longer winning, but now we were police blotter material. The worst, however, remained to be seen.

On April 25, 2007 everything changed. For Michael Vick. For the Falcons franchise. For our dreams of Super Bowl glory. Officials, investigating Vick's cousin, searched his property in Virginia, uncovering evidence of a dog fighting ring. Initially denying it, Vick was later arrested on felony charges. He was sentenced and served almost two years in jail. *Strike Three.* And there it was, the end of the Michael Vick era in Atlanta. We hardly knew you. Almost over before it ever really got started. Michael Vick had gone from penthouse to penitentiary. He traded his top-selling Falcons jersey for the latest in prison wear fashion.

The Curse had struck again. The creativity in which our teams were now being undone had reached new levels of absurdity. An entire era of promise brought to its knees by dog fighting? Really? Certainly, no other city could lay claim to a such an embarrassment. Again, we were able to add to the "only in Atlanta" list. As in, only in Atlanta can a franchise be decimated by its star quarterback being arrested for dog fighting. Incredible. Remember, James Cameron can't write this stuff. The Curse can never be accused of copying someone else's work; he is the true originator of it all. And it is quite original.

Six years prior, the Falcons had drafted their supposed savior. Now, he was no more. His story had been written. Felonies - 1. Championships - 0. He was not Michael Jordan. He was not Tiger Woods. However, he was just the latest chapter in a long line of Atlanta fiascos. On that draft night in 2001, had I been asked to predict the future of Michael Vick, the list of predictions surely would have included Super Bowls, MVP awards, and plenty of record-breaking moments. I'm pretty confident felony charges for dog fighting would not have made the list. Plenty of athletes have been taken down in their primes, over the years, for different indiscretions. Shoeless Joe Jackson's career was infamously derailed due to gambling habits, but that has been the downfall of many athletes. Dwight "Doc" Gooden never reached immortal status because of his drug addiction. However, that can be said of many.

No one, and I mean absolutely no one, has had their career stripped away for something as peculiarly unique as Michael Vick. And to make matters worse, do you remember how we "plundered and pillaged" the San Diego Chargers in that 2001 draft? Well, I think they did all right for themselves. In 2001, we traded a treasure trove worth of draft assets for Vick. All the Chargers did that same year was draft two future Hall of Famers, running back LaDainian Tomlinson and quarterback Drew Brees. Yep, we definitely got the best of 'em. On top of that, Brees is still flinging it around, some eighteen years later, throwing daggers into the hearts of every Atlanta fan as a Super Bowl champion and member of our bitter rival, the New Orleans Saints.

As unbelievable as all of that may seem, believe it or not, the *Greatest Hits* album for the Curse had yet to be recorded.

Chapter 11

Salsa With A Side Of Curse

    The Atlanta Falcons had their chances, but to no avail. However, football in the state of Georgia was not dead. In my household, we bled red and black, much like 99% of the state. The University of Georgia football team had pretty much been out the national limelight for twenty years, but under new coach Mark Richt, they were back on center stage. Nothing brings our state together quite like when the Dawgs are really good. And in 2002, they were. Behind the efforts of the Davids, Pollack and Greene, Georgia had found themselves back in the hunt, ranked fourth in the nation. At 8-0, if UGA had won out, they almost certainly would have played for the national championship.

    On November 2, Georgia played Florida in what is known as The World's Largest Outdoor Cocktail Party. Every year, the Bulldogs and Gators square off in Jacksonville, for what had become a one-sided affair. Over a 21-year stretch the Gators were an astonishing 18-3 against Georgia. Can you call it a rivalry when you've only won three times in two decades? However, in 2002, things appeared as if they would be different. Georgia went into the game undefeated, whereas the Gators were an underwhelming 5-3. Sounds like an easy win for the championship-bound Dawgs. Right? Understand this, against Florida, nothing was ever easy. This would be no different. The game was a back and forth affair, with Georgia leading 13-12 midway through the third quarter and driving. On third down at Florida's 18-yard line, I saw one of the strangest and inexplicable plays. After Greene threw an incomplete pass, offensive lineman George Foster appeared to have landed on a Gator defensive lineman. However, Foster didn't get off, and then appeared to intentionally bounce up and down on the Gator multiple times. He just kept bouncing. This, in spite of the referee's best efforts to extricate Foster from the Gator's "personal space". Eventually, the official had no choice but to throw a flag. The personal foul penalty backed the Bulldogs up fifteen yards, leaving them with around a 50-yard field goal attempt. As one could almost predict in situations like these, the kick banged off the goal post and missed. Florida stole away with the momentum, riding it to a 20-13 lead.

With a little more than two minutes remaining, though, Georgia had one last chance. With the Bulldogs running out of opportunities, unbelievably, Georgia appeared to have a great one. Wide receiver Terrence Edwards had broken wide open down the middle of the field. He was WIDE OPEN, no Gator within ten yards, and surely about to score the game-tying touchdown. Only he didn't. Edwards dropped the pass, Georgia lost the game by one score, and their season was effectively over.

Clearly the more talented team, the Bulldogs, unimaginably, failed on all of its thirteen third down attempts. Succeed on even 3 or 4 of those and we probably win the game. But we didn't. To make matters worse, three other undefeated teams lost that week, meaning the Dawgs would have vaulted towards the top of the rankings had they been victorious. UGA coming close, only to have our hearts ripped out, would be a common theme during the Mark Richt era.

In 2007, Georgia lost two games early, but rallied and was arguably the hottest team in the country towards the end of the season. If we had gotten to the SEC Championship Game and won, we would have very likely coasted to the championship against an inferior Ohio State team. Strangely enough, it all came down to a game between Tennessee and Kentucky. How was the Bulldogs' fate intertwined with these two teams, you ask? If Kentucky was to somehow defeat Tennessee, Georgia would win the SEC East. Odds were long against that happening, though, as Tennessee was the heavy favorite.

I remember this game like it was yesterday. My brothers and our families were eating out at a Mexican restaurant, watching the game on the big screen. Who knew this game would be so exciting? My burrito was the last thing on my mind. I'm pretty sure the entire restaurant had guacamole churning in their stomach as Kentucky lined up for a chip-shot field goal to win the game. Everything had gone exactly as we had needed. We couldn't believe it. Kentucky was about to win, sending Georgia back into the championship hunt.

In life, you learn to rely on empirical evidence. I know if I jump up, I will come back down. I know if I hit my head on a wall, it will hurt. I know if I stand in the rain, I will get wet. Surely, empirical evidence should have led me to a simple conclusion, as Kentucky lined up for what amounted to an extra point. I had been down this road before with teams in every sport. Of course, I was nervous with anticipation, but, honestly, I was already planning on eating a celebration taco. However, Tecumseh reached his hand up and blocked the kick. Okay, it wasn't Tecumseh, but it might as well have been. The game ended with a Tennessee win, leaving us all to shed proverbial tears into our salsa. This was one of those moments that lingers in your thoughts for a long time. The "what might have been" thoughts are unavoidable. The "why can't it ever be our lucky day" mantra started up again in earnest. But, in truth, why is it never our lucky day? Why does the sun always shine on our opponent? Even in a game that was not involving one of our teams, the result was a disappointment. Georgia did not go on to play for the championship, but they did continue their torrid run through to the end of the season. When all was said and done, however, the Bulldogs ended this year just like all of the others – not ranked #1.

It was a painful few years watching the Dawgs. They had the talent to win every year, but didn't. We were seemingly never able to put ourselves in position late in the season. Every year seemed to begin with a loss, due to early season suspensions from off-the-field incidents. This seemed to bite us in the behind every year. Every year until 2012.

This was the year that the Curse became a tangible, living, breathing entity. As a sports community, we had seen it all. Or so we thought. We were about to begin classes at Tecumseh University, majoring in the Curse.

As 2012 wound down, UGA had advanced to the SEC Championship Game ranked third in the country. Their opponent was the Alabama Crimson Tide, a team that will haunt us for years to come. A win in this game, and Georgia was assured of a National Championship opportunity against the Notre Dame Fighting Irish. History will go on to show that the 2012 Notre Dame squad was incredibly overrated. With that said, everyone in the country thought this SEC title matchup to be the de facto National Championship Game, with the game against the Irish a mere formality. Not only that, the game was in our backyard, the Georgia Dome. Certainly, the crowd was going to be very pro-Dawgs. And it was.

Alabama was the top-ranked team in the country, and should have been, considering they had won two out of the last three titles. For Crimson Tide fans, the Bulldogs were just a stepping stone to another championship. However, these Dawgs came to play. These Dawgs were hungry. And these Dawgs were beating Alabama in the third quarter.

Let me set the stage. I had spent the better part of eight years of marriage trying to get my wife, Misty, hooked on the Bulldogs. This was the year I finally had some success. And of all the seasons to rope her in, this appeared to be the best. Hook her in during a championship run and she'll never get out. The plan was perfect, and Georgia was holding up their end of the bargain.

Midway through the third quarter Georgia was up by four, with Alabama lining up to kick a field goal and the momentum clearly on our side. I looked over to Misty and ushered forth my inner Nostradamus, as I'm sure many fans did at the same moment. I stated the obvious, "We really need to block this kick." The next play is the type of play the Curse thrives on. Alabama snapped the ball, up went the 49-yard attempt, and BOOM. Georgia blocked the kick, Bulldog Alec Ogletree scooped it up and raced down the remainder of the field to score, what I thought, was a decisive touchdown. Without thinking, I grabbed my wife, lifted her up in the air and screamed in utter exultation, "We're going to play for National Championship!"

Can we just pause for a minute right here? I know, I know. What on earth was I thinking? Did I really say what I think I just said? Did I really just pull the traditional celebratory "wife lift"? In that split second of unbridled joy, I neglected to remember where I lived and who I was cheering for. This play was no different than Terry Pendleton's double in the 1991 World Series, or Francisco

Cabrera's game-winning hit for the Braves in the 1992 NLCS, or Morten Andersen's NFC Championship overtime kick in 1999. In those moments of pure ecstasy, ever so brief as they may be, you forget. You forget our history. You forget it's "never over 'til it's over". And worst of all, you forget about the Curse.

Somehow, my emotions always get the best of me. For some reason, though, this play felt different. This time I just knew we had dealt the death blow, as the Georgia Dome crowd was going absolutely bonkers. There seemed no way Bama was going to recover. And yet they did. Why does every game of this magnitude have to turn out exactly the same way? Can't we just win and that's that? At some point, don't some of these games have to break our way? Well, this was not the game for things to start evening out.

Yes, the momentum was all Georgia's way. And then it wasn't. Within two and a half minutes, the Tide had scored a touchdown and succeeded on a two-point conversion. I've been a connoisseur of football for a long time and seen plenty of two-point conversions. I am also fully aware that the success rate of such an attempt is no more than a fifty-fifty chance, but it sure seems, in games like these, the other team is successful almost every time. Just like that (fingers snapped), Alabama was right back in it. Then, just a few minutes later, they had taken the lead. The premature "wife lift" seemed like a lifetime ago. As the Tide scored to take the lead, my wife actually said I had jinxed us. Perhaps I had. Was it my fault? Was it somebody else's fault? Does it really matter?

However, as I've said, our Curse is more nuanced than to let the game get away from us that easily. As if expected, Georgia came back to take the lead 28-25. Not only that, they forced a Bama punt and had the ball with a chance to run out the clock. If ever there was a running back to run the clock out, we had him – Todd Gurley. Gurley was most likely the best running back in the country, and we were about to ride his legs to championship glory. Georgia had a third down and ONE YARD to go with only a little over five minutes remaining. One yard to go, with Todd Gurley at running back. Out of all the plays in the game, in my opinion, this was the biggest one. However, as always seems to be the case, the biggest play of the game never turns out the way we hope. One yard away from being able to bleed whatever little time was left off the clock. One yard away from putting another nail in Alabama's coffin.

    Unfortunately, that one yard was tougher to get than we all had hoped. Gurley was stuffed on third down and Georgia had to punt. We had given those guys another chance. Where they had little chance, they now had new life. After a couple of plays, Bama risked a run on third down and five. As you may have guessed, they got it. They got exactly five yards. Of course they did. Did we really expect anything less? I looked at my wife and again spoke prophetic words. I said, "Georgia better be careful, Alabama's setting us up for a dagger here." On cue, Bama quarterback A.J. McCarron threw a deep 45-yard touchdown pass to receiver Amari Cooper. Bama led. Every big moment goes for the other guys. Every time. That is a truism around here. They say you make your own breaks in a game, but sometimes every team needs a little luck. Well, we never get it.

    Through all of that, Georgia miraculously found its way back down the field to the Alabama 8-yard line, with 15 seconds remaining and the clock running. Just spike the ball and we get two (or three) cracks at the endzone for the win. It's at this point, where it would probably be useful to remind everyone of that seemingly insignificant two-point play for Alabama earlier in the game. Had they missed it,

Georgia would have been in perfect position for a short field goal and the win. Or, had Bama simply kicked the extra point, Georgia would surely be lining up for the game-tying field goal. However, they did get the two points, and that is the primary reason the next play turned out the way it did.

At the Tide 8-yard-line, all the Bulldogs had to do was spike the ball to give themselves a couple of legitimate touchdown attempts. JUST SPIKE THE BALL. As you may have guessed, however, Georgia quarterback Aaron Murray did not spike the ball. Instead he rushed to the line, bled off our own precious seconds from the clock and flung a hurried pass that was tipped by an Alabama defender. As the ball floated for what seemed like an eternity, it safely landed in the arms of a Bulldog. Only one problem, that Bulldog was at the 5-yard line. The ball was caught, time ran out and the game had ended.

Like we had done many times before, we sat in stunned silence. Was it really over? Are there no more chances? We were facing the all-too-familiar feeling of finality. A finality that meant your chances were finished and you had lost. You sit there for the next few minutes (hours? days?) replaying every opportunity lost, every turning point. You invariably end up realizing that had just a single play broken our way, the game would have been ours. Just any one play. Yet, every play of consequence went the wrong way. Every play that could have determined the outcome went how Alabama needed it to. How does that happen? Why does that always happen? That dreaded Curse had its way with us once more. It drew us in and crushed us. It gave us hope as great as hope could be, while still coming up short. You'd almost rather have lost the game by thirty, than to suffer through this. Not again.

As expected, Alabama faced Notre Dame for the National Championship. And, as expected, the game was over before it even got started. The Tide were up two touchdowns after the first quarter; up four touchdowns by halftime. All I could think about while watching that game was "This should have been us." There was little doubt the outcome of that game would have been the same had it been Georgia, instead of Alabama. It was going to be our National Championship. We would have been the team on top in the end. All eyes would have been on us (for more than the usual coming up short). However, it was not us. It never is. The Curse was just beginning the torture. And we had no idea how torturous things would actually get.

Chapter 12

Almost...Again

 The first thirty-seven years of my life as a sports fan were highly unfulfilling. We were presented with chance after chance, only cashing it in that one time in 1995. However, you realize the more close calls you have, the more you want it. 2012 was a signature year for our local sports scene. However, it may have also been the signature year for our beloved Curse. It seemed as if we had a championship run in each sport, to go along with a memorable Curse moment. Looking back, the intensity may have been unlike any other year in our state's sports history.

 I can remember listening to local sports talk radio one particular afternoon in late September. The day's topic focused on asking the listeners which area team they thought might win a championship first. The community was abuzz. For sports fans, we were like kids in a candy store and the options were plentiful. Whatever satisfied your sweet tooth was readily available. Braves. Falcons. Dawgs. Surely, one of our teams would capitalize. Maybe two. Who knows, we thought, maybe this was the year that everything finally began to even out and we win all three. In 1969-70, New York pulled off such a feat. The Miracle Mets won the World Series, the Jets pulled off one of the biggest upsets in history to win the Super Bowl, and the

Knicks were the toast of Madison Square Garden for winning the NBA title. Why not us? We were certainly due. Overdue. In the span of four months, our city witnessed more postseason tension and excitement than we had seen from the inaugural 1966 season through 1990, combined. I couldn't wait to wake up each morning to read the daily news, to hear the latest hot takes, or to watch the most recent do-or-die game.

As a kid, I remember my father reading the sports page each day. As you'd expect, he had "first dibs". My brother and I waited eagerly for him to fold it up and set it aside. This meant it was up for the taking. It wouldn't be long before it was in one of our possession. At that time, my Braves were a last place team, the Falcons were perennial losers, and the Bulldogs and Hawks were good, but not great. Even still, I relished reading through the sports news of the day. I poured over box scores like I was studying for the Bar Exam. I could tell you every detail, every statistic about players and teams. I'm sure my passion for statistics began curled up on my living room floor reading every line of the Atlanta Journal Constitution sports section. Fast forward twenty-five years later and I still felt like that boy waiting for my father to give up the literary gold. Only, my teams weren't bottom dwellers anymore, they were league leaders, with championship aspirations. It was all-consuming. It was amazing. By year's end, I think we were all completely and thoroughly wiped out, yet somehow energized.

After UGA lost the golden opportunity for triumph in 2012, it struck me how much winning it all would have actually meant. Maybe, it's that as you get older, you begin to truly understand how difficult championships are to come by. You see other cities and other fan bases celebrating with regularity, not appreciating what they have. You almost wonder what it's like to get so desensitized to winning. Surely, WE would savor every second of every play of an entire season that ended in a title. At least, that's what I keep telling my myself.

Watching Alabama beat Georgia, then finish off Notre Dame for their third title in four years hit me harder (and differently) than ever before. It absolutely stirred something within me. Before 2012, my heart was on a string that rose and fell with every sports season. Since that year, however, I would describe it more as a craving that can only be satiated by a championship. A craving that grows by the passing of each season. The excitement I felt as Alec Ogletree was returning the blocked kick against Alabama had rekindled that passion within me. That nearly unrivaled feeling of "we're about to be champions" revealed itself, once again. As Ogletree crossed the goal line, sending all of Georgia into absolute pandemonium, we all felt it. However, we also felt the usual anguish that follows our jubilation, leaving the whole lot of us thoroughly despondent. THAT is the Curse at its best (or worst).

I'll admit it, the Braves of the 90's absconded with much of my sports fervor, as did the debacles of the Falcons' Super Bowl and Georgia's "almosts" of 2002 and 2007. However, those few months in 2012 brought it all back. And then some. If everyone in Georgia was being completely honest with themselves, they would admit it was different for them as well. We were all now on a championship quest, not for our own selfish desires, but for our collective sports soul. Somehow, this all became bigger than us. I needed it. Our city needed it. The state needed it. Can an entire state have a championship mission? If so, we were all on it. An entire state ready to raise our banner. It had to happen, for all of our sakes. On cue, just a little over a month after the Georgia-Alabama game, we were at it again. Another opportunity laying right at our feet, while the Curse lay in wait, like a lion preparing to pounce. Unfortunately, we were the prey.

The fall of 2012 also gave us an exquisite season from the Atlanta Falcons. For the second time in three years they ended the regular season as the best team in the league, finishing 13-3 and earning a first round bye in the playoffs. The Falcons had it clicking on all cylinders, to say the least. When you are the top seed in the league, there are obvious expectations that go along with that. Our expectation was Super Bowl Championship. After coming so tantalizingly close with the Georgia Bulldogs just a month earlier, we were ready for redemption. In our minds, however, we all wondered if redemption was truly attainable. We knew the Curse was real, but we were about to find out precisely how cutthroat it actually was.

In the divisional playoff game against the rising Seattle Seahawks, the Falcons jumped out to a commanding 20-0 lead at home in the Georgia Dome. Big lead, huh. Sound familiar? Midway through the third quarter the lead was still twenty, the score 27-7. What occurred over the next quarter and half should have been recognized for what it was, an omen of things to come. The Seahawks stormed back into the game and unbelievably took a 28-27 lead with only 34 seconds remaining in the game. There it was. The Curse had bitten us again. Only in Atlanta could we blow a twenty-point second half lead. Sports writers all over town were preparing their epitaphs for the Falcons season. This was typical and it sounded all too familiar. Remember, however, this Curse was out for blood. Losing a measly divisional round game, although painful as a number one seed, wouldn't be too difficult to get over. In fact, the Falcons did it two seasons earlier. Thirteen regular season wins. First round bye. Home playoff game. And a 48-21 trouncing at the hands of the Green Bay Packers. Yikes.

It sure appeared as though we had suffered another "typical Atlanta" loss. Only it wasn't. The Falcons got the ball right back down the field and kicked a go-ahead field goal with only eight seconds left. Now, I will tell you that we actually did win this game, but even then, we did everything we could to lose. All we had to do was kick the ball deep and the game would essentially be over. That's too easy for us, right? Falcons coach Mike Smith decided to get cute and "squib" kick the ball, supposedly to negate any chance for a Seattle kick return (even though only one kickoff had been returned throughout the game). Great idea, Coach Smith.

We have been on the wrong side of history one too many times when it comes to poor coaching decisions. This was another. The squib kick went exactly 19 yards. NINETEEN yards. The Seahawks downed the ball at midfield with six seconds still remaining. Are you kidding me? That's almost field goal range. At the very least, we just gift-wrapped Seattle a free Hail Mary pass attempt, along with a chance to steal back the game. This would certainly have gone down as one of the worst collapses in sports history (Oh, don't worry, we'll make sure to corner the market on those, as well).

Fortunately, for the love of all that's good in the world, we intercepted their desperation attempt and secured a trip to the NFC Championship Game. A game that would be played in our own back yard. A back yard in which the Falcons had gone 8-1 thus far during the 2012 season. It was looking good on all fronts. Perhaps we finally overcame a Curse moment, and that alone would carry us to the title……. Yeah right. What book have you been reading? Hadn't we learned yet? The Curse only gives, so that it can take away.

In the NFC title match, Atlanta was facing off against the San Francisco 49ers. For once, could we just make this game easy? For once, couldn't we just be the dominant team that cruises to an easy win? For once, couldn't we just keep my heart out my throat and enjoy a victory lap? Not these Falcons. Not this city. Not ever.

In Atlanta, we have lost the big games in so many different ways. There have been horrendous coaching decisions (Oh, have there ever), physical errors, mental mistakes, and some of the most stupefying bad luck in recorded history. However, the most wretched way to lose is choking up a big lead. This is the last thing a sports town wants to be known for, yet that is exactly what has happened for us. Being a poor frontrunner is certainly not the best claim to fame.

They say Tiger Woods doesn't win majors if he's trailing on Sunday. Who cares? When he's leading, he holds on. And he's led a lot. I'd call that a great frontrunner. The Boston Celtics were historically known to be invincible at home in Game Seven. You know why they were always at home? They were good. That's a great frontrunner. One of my favorite photos is of superhorse Secretariat's jockey Ron Turcotte looking over his shoulder at the Belmont Stakes. This third leg of the 1973 triple crown chase saw Secretariat win the race by THIRTY-ONE lengths. When Turcotte looked back, he saw no challengers. You know why? His horse was, perhaps, the greatest of all frontrunners.

The difference between the truly great and everyone else – the great teams know how to close it out. They have learned how to cut the head off the snake. If you give a team life, when there seemed to be none, they usually end up surviving longer than you. That's what happened to Georgia against Bama. And they wouldn't be the last.

On January 20, 2013, the Falcons played host to the 49ers in another attempt to bring a Super Bowl trophy to Atlanta. It sure looked like the Falcons were going to run away with this one, but as we know, big leads in Atlanta are like the sands of time – they keep slipping away. In an instant, the Falcons were up 17-0, one play into the second quarter. Observed history tells us 17-0 is the type of lead that generally leads to celebrations. That is, the observed history from anywhere else. Not here.

I've got to be honest here. After Falcons tight end Tony Gonzalez hauled in a touchdown late in the first half, I did what I promised myself I'd never do again. I lifted my wife and said, "we're going to the Super Bowl!" I know, not the wife lift again. After seeing so many collapses over the years, including one just a month earlier, I still fell victim to premature celebrating. What force of nature keeps causing me to do this? I literally can't help myself. Perhaps it's because I want it so bad. Perhaps I just love lifting my wife. Although, how many of you wouldn't have had similar thoughts of bliss under the same circumstances? Come on, there was absolutely no way we would have a second collapse within a month. But……

In the third quarter, the 49ers were predictably chipping away, eventually cutting the lead to 24-21. As leads start dwindling, it seems as though the noose really tightens. You start playing "not to lose", rather than trying to win. You start making blunders not typical of the play that got you to that point. That was certainly the case in this game. After San Francisco had cut the lead to three, Atlanta drove right back down the field. However, quarterback Matt Ryan threw an interception at the 49ers' 38-yard-line. Wasted opportunity. On their next possession, the Falcons drove again with ease, this time reaching the 49ers' 28-yard-line. If nothing else, they were already in prime field goal position. However, Ryan had the shotgun snap go right through his dainty fingertips, resulting in a fumble. To me, of all the plays that determined the outcome, this was the most impactful. Every big game has that moment when you look back and say, "That was the one." The one play that turns the fate of players and franchises. And somehow, those plays are always at the expense of Atlanta. Improbable, but true. Matt Ryan's fumble turned what would have at least been a field goal, very possibly more, into another lifeline tossed to the 49ers. It's not uncommon for a fumble to be the biggest play of the game. But a fumble where the quarterback isn't even touched? Really? A fumble on a perfect snap, when there was no pressure or reason to feel rushed? I couldn't get the picture of the ball glancing off Ryan's hands, along with his feeble attempt to jump on the ball, out of my mind. A score would have meant so much at this juncture of the game. Unfortunately, Matty Ice's hands were as slippery as his nickname.

There are certain plays that occur in a game when you say to yourself, "Now, we're going to lose." We've seen those plays too often not to notice them when they appear. They never fail to appear, and each time is like a dagger to the heart. Even as you continue to watch the game and hope for the desired result, you continually think back to those plays and how things could have been different. Yes, the game had another quarter remaining, but that fumble would have lasting ramifications.

Midway through the fourth, the Falcons forced a 49ers fumble just as they were going in for the go-ahead score. Normally, that would be a game-changing, momentum-changing play. But this was Atlanta. A play like that crush would've crushed our soul, but it seemed to buoy our opponent. San Francisco's own fumble only served to delay the inevitable, as they scored to take the lead just 5 minutes later anyway. Atlanta got the ball back, down by four. Imagine if Ryan hadn't fumbled and we had kicked the field goal, instead. Down by four, however, we needed a touchdown to win. Nothing else would help.

If anyone is keeping score, consider the Georgia-Alabama game for one moment. The Bulldogs were also driving at the end of the game down by four. Down by four, needing a touchdown to win. Down by four in the prelude game to the championship. Down by four in a game played at the Georgia Dome, in front of a mostly partisan crowd, driving to the same endzone as the Falcons.

If anyone does not think the Curse of Tecumseh is real, please look at Exhibit A. Coincidences such as this should be seen as being much more than…..well………coincidences. It's more than merely an uncanny fluke. It's fate. It's destiny. It's kismet. The Curse is real and it's toying with us. The Curse is real, and it's enjoying every second of our angst. THE CURSE IS REAL. Can we all finally agree upon this and just move on? Atlanta stood no more chance of winning than the Georgia Bulldogs did. The Curse would not allow it. Early in this final drive, Ryan found receiver Harry Douglas streaking wide-open down the sideline. The pass was perfect, right in stride. Only, just before Douglas was able to make the catch and run it in for the uncontested go-ahead touchdown, he inexplicably stumbled. What? How?

Yep, the play that should have put the Falcons on top, perhaps for good, ended with Douglas falling to the turf for an innocent 22-yard gain. Was anybody else looking at his feet? I'm pretty sure I saw Tecumseh reach a hand up from beneath and gently trip the receiver. That's the only explanation. Athletes of this caliber simply don't just stumble. Yet, he did. Of course, he did. Despite that, the Falcons continued the drive. Although, did anyone think they would actually win? Chance after chance after chance had gone by the wayside. You just can't keep wasting opportunities. Yet, for some reason, as the Falcons faced fourth down from inside San Francisco's 10-yard line, I still held my breath in hope and anticipation of something wondrous happening. The feeling was eerily familiar, as UGA had been in the exact same position. As Matt Ryan's last gasp pass to receiver Roddy White fell incomplete, all of Atlanta had that same sense of finality as we had felt a month earlier, following the SEC Championship.

Both games went down to the wire. Both games saw my team have a real chance in the end to make that one memorable, my-life-will-forever-now-be-complete play. Yet, neither team did. Both games ended with loss, when victory had seemed certain. Both teams were on the wrong side of every big play in the second half. Both seasons ended in bitter disappointment. Both seasons ended with the largest of pits in all of our stomachs. Such symmetry. Such agony. Agony is losing both games after having double-digit second half leads. Agony is having knowledge of how difficult it is to make it that far, only to go home with nothing to show for it. Agony is believing that no matter what your teams do, they have no shot at being the last ones standing. Autumn of 2012 began with dreams of glory, yet ended in a nightmare. We had all awakened in a cold sweat, utterly shaken by what had transpired. The Curse was beginning to take on a life of its own. It had grown to epic proportions. And you know what? Neither of those games represented the most heinous moment of the Curse in 2012. No, that honor occurred somewhere between third base and left field.

Chapter 13

Groundhog Day

If the Braves of the 90's were underachieving, what do you consider the Braves of the 2000's? Let's put things into perspective. The five teams with the most playoff appearances this century are the Yankees (16 appearances), the Cardinals (13), the Braves (11), the Dodgers (11) and the Red Sox (10). Simply looking at this statistic might lead one to believe the Braves have been right in the thick of it every year. Now, consider this. The Yankees have 4 World Series appearances, with 2 titles. The Cardinals have reached 4 World Series, winning 2. The Red Sox have reached 4 World Series, winning all 4 times. Even the Dodgers, who have no titles to show for their efforts, have graced the World Series stage twice. The Braves? You guessed it, ZERO World Series titles in ZERO appearances. Throw in the San Francisco Giants' 7 playoff seasons, 4 World Series appearances, and 3 titles just for good measure.

Think about it. The Braves have made the anything-can-happen-in-any-given-year baseball playoffs ELEVEN times this century and have absolutely no World Series appearances. For comparison, the Kansas City Royals have made the playoffs exactly twice over that same span and have made TWO World Series, winning it once. Okay, okay, but at least Atlanta has probably made several

League Championship Series. Right? Well, not exactly. They have reached only one NLCS, way back in 2001.

Wait a second. Doesn't it only take winning one round in the baseball playoffs to reach the League Championship Series? That's right. We have not won a single series since 2001, despite making the playoffs in half of the seasons. Consider the 90's Braves again. From 1991-1999 the Braves played in all eight postseasons (1994 season was cancelled due to labor issues). In those eight years they made the World Series five times, winning it once. We thought THAT was bad. We didn't know how good we had it, choking in the World Series every year. At least we were there. As a fan, we hated Kent Hrbek or Jim Leyritz. At least there was a Kent Hrbek or Jim Leyritz.

I'm about to say a most unbelievable, unthinkable, unfathomable statistic. Beginning with that 2001 season, the Braves have lost 10 consecutive playoff series. TEN. As if it needs to be said, that is the most consecutive series without a win, tying the record previously held by those once-cursed Cubs. Those Cubs, however, spread their streak over a nearly one-hundred-year stretch. The Braves have accomplished this feat of ignominy in just nineteen seasons. They say baseball series are like a coin flip - you never know on which side the coin will land. Well, in that case, I challenge anyone to flip a coin ten times and get heads up on ten consecutive flips. Nearly impossible. Yet, the Braves have achieved the nearly impossible. Every year we enter the playoffs with the highest of hopes, and every year our season is over before we even blink. Losing is bad. Losing agonizingly is worse. But this?

After losing to the Arizona Diamondbacks in the 2001 NLCS, the Braves began this long run of one and done. In 2002, 2003 and 2004, the Braves were defeated in the first round Division Series by losing winner-take-all

Game Five at home each year. In those three seasons, the Braves won 101, 101 and 96 games, respectively. Every year we were the better team. Every year we would lose the first game of the series, putting our backs against the wall almost immediately. Every year we played the deciding game in our home park. Every year we lost in heartbreaking fashion. Every year the losses became more preposterous.

Then, in 2005, we had a resounding last blow to our 14 consecutive division title run. Yes, again, we won the division, but not quite as comfortably. In the Division Series playoff round against the Astros, the Braves lost Game One at home, again. Same story. In Game Four with Atlanta down two games to one, it looked like we were sending the series back home for ANOTHER Game Five winner-take-all matchup. The Braves were up 6-1 in the eighth inning and cruising to an even series. In complete honesty, I left my television with the game 6-1, to go play some pickup basketball with my brothers, with another Game Five in Atlanta assured. Or so I thought. Winning a playoff game leaves you in such a wonderfully relaxed mood. Thank goodness, I went to the gym before I heard the result. I actually enjoyed myself. Upon leaving my temporary frivolity, I turned on my car radio to listen to some postgame excitement. Only, there was no excitement. My wonderfully relaxed mood was gone. The game, which I had left two hours earlier, was still in progress. How was that possible? Unfortunately, Atlanta had given up a grand slam in the eighth, reducing the lead to a single run. Then, with two outs in the ninth, the Astros hit a game tying homer.

In that moment, I was reminded of Atlanta's putrid sports history. Losing the 6-0 lead to the Yankees in 1996 obviously came to mind. This one, however, seemed different. This one didn't just smell like another blown opportunity and the end of another series. This one felt like the end of an era. All the years, all the chances, and all of the collapses had come down to this. The game would continue without scoring for the next eight innings. The Astros went hitless inning after inning, yet the Braves could never capitalize on scoring opportunities. Typical.

As you watch these games, you feel fate doing its familiar thing. You expect the inevitable botched play, missed call, or regrettable Bobby Cox decision. They always appeared in some form or fashion. Was Scott Leius ready to hit another improbable home run? Was Pete Incaviglia about to make another unlikely run-saving diving catch? Was Eric Gregg about to call strike three on another pitch closer to the on deck circle than it was to home plate? Every Astros hitless inning only served to make the anticipated dramatic Braves loss just a little more dramatic. Let's don't "just lose", let's break a few records while doing so. This time we broke the record for the longest postseason game in history. This had loss written all over it for seasoned Atlanta fans. Steven Spielberg should come and sit at the feet of the Curse to learn about surprising the viewer. Stephen King should take notes on thrillingly cruel plot twists.

The game played on into the eighteenth inning, Roger Clemens pitching relief for Houston. The Braves produced Joey Devine from their bullpen. Clemens and his eventual 354 career wins against Devine and his 8 career wins. If the teams were reversed, Braves fans would say the opponent had the advantage (see Greg Maddux vs. Livan Hernandez in 1997). We always had a knack of making the underdog appear to be a world beater. This, however, turned out as most would have expected. Roger Clemens added to his legend and Devine was never heard of again after serving up the game-winning homerun in the decisive eighteenth inning. This was a capstone loss for the Braves and their 14-year division run. With one swing of the bat, Houston ended the most glorious stretch in Atlanta Braves history. The most glorious and most frustrating. It was over and it all came crashing down in predictable fashion. To this day, it's tough going to Braves games and seeing all of the pennants hanging, recognizing division crowns. To me, they only represent coming up short of the ultimate prize year after year. Still, after the run was over, the Braves kept coming back. Though, nothing quite like the streak of those 14 consecutive division titles.

The Atlanta Braves remind me of the movie *Groundhog Day*. Phil Connor, a bitter curmudgeon of a weatherman, keeps reliving the same day of February 2 over and over again in the quaint town of Punxsutawney, PA. As the days mount for Connor, so do the frustrations. The frustration of his circumstance. The frustration over his miserable existence. The frustration with who he's become versus who he wants to be. No matter what he does, it's always the same result. Phil was seemingly unable to break free from the inescapable truth, the dark reality of who he really is.

Similarly, the Braves, at least since 2001, have been reliving the same day over and over again. Ten times they have reached postseason play. Ten times they have lost Game One (another record, by the way). Ten times they have lost the series. Every year, same result. We can't change it. The struggle is fruitless. We will seemingly never be able to break free from our own dark reality. The Curse will be victorious. And it will always be victorious.......... until it isn't. Let it be noted that Phil Connor finally struck all the right chords, eventually waking up to a glorious new first day of the rest of his life. That begs the question - will we ever wake up to a different reality, our own "new day"?

Every year the Braves reached the playoffs, only to lose on a different twist of fate. In 2010, with all-stars Chipper Jones and Martin Prado injured, fill-in Brooks Conrad was forced into the limelight. Not only were the Braves making this playoff venture without their best offensive players, they were reduced to playing the weak-fielding Conrad. In Game Three of the Division Series, the Braves led the pivotal game 2-1 in the bottom of the ninth, unhittable Craig Kimbrel in to close out the game. As we probably should have expected, it wasn't that easy. It never is. Predictably, Conrad made his third error of the game, allowing the winning run to score, in an eventual 3-2 loss. Every turning point game comes down to moments like this and there is always a Brooks Conrad there to do us in. The 2010 playoffs gave us another Game One failure, another moment of incredulity, three more one-run losses and another series defeat.

In 2011, the Braves actually didn't make the playoffs. The only problem with that is they should have. On September 6, the Braves had an 8.5 game lead over the St. Louis Cardinals (those guys again?) for the wild card spot in the playoffs. This was a cinch. In the bag. The fat-lady-has-already-sung-type of lead. In fact, this would be the largest lead EVER lost this late in the season if the Braves did, in fact, blow it. Well, this is Atlanta, isn't it? We only lose while breaking records, right? You can probably guess what's about to happen.

On September 9, we were still up by 7.5 games over the Cardinals. On top of that, we were playing the first of three games against those same Cardinals. On top of that, we were leading the first game of the series 3-1 in the ninth inning with Rookie of the Year Kimbrel on the mound. It needs to be noted that Kimbrel was incredible that season, collecting 46 saves, including 25 consecutive saves coming into this game. There was no other player in baseball you wanted pitching in that situation. We were three outs away from putting the death knell on the Cardinals. Win this game and St. Louis will most likely lose any hope of coming back with only three weeks left. Win this game and the Cardinals probably roll over and die in the next two games, while the Braves can begin preparing for their next first round postseason series loss. However, that is not what happened. Kimbrel blew the save. Of course he did. The Cardinals fueled by their late-game heroics won the next two games of the series. Of course they did. And the race was on.

Atlanta continually had chance after chance to end this playoff chase, but never could. On September 19, still with a three-game lead, the Braves were beating the Florida Marlins 5-4 with two outs in the ninth inning. TWO OUTS. NOBODY ON. CRAIG KIMBREL PITCHING. Yep, sure seems like a Curse moment if I ever saw one. Marlin Emilio Bonifacio hit a game-ending weak ground ball to Chipper Jones. Unfortunately, for Braves fans it wasn't game-ending. Of all the times, in all of the moments, Jones lost sight of the ground ball in the stadium lights. What? I've heard of losing sight of a fly ball in the lights, but a grounder? Bonifacio miraculously reached first base. Nice job, Curse. Two pitches later, former Brave Omar Infante hit a game-winning homerun, obliterating a Braves celebration that was certain just seconds earlier. It was another "you had to see it to believe it" moment. Oh, we believed it. It was the Curse at its best and we were all dedicated believers.

The playoff race went down to the last game of the year. The Braves and Cardinals were now tied on the final day. The Cardinals, having already won their game, were watching the Braves against the Phillies. Atlanta actually led this game in the ninth 3-2, but as happened too often in September, Kimbrel blew the save. The Phillies tied the game, sending it to extra innings. We've been down this road so many times. Inning after inning, we kept waiting for the other shoe to drop. We knew it was just a matter of time before the Phillies scored the go-ahead run. It was always fated to happen. We pretended to have hope as we watched the game progress, but in our hearts we knew it was another fait accompli. And it was. The Phillies won it in the thirteenth inning, ending the game, as well as the Braves season. The September collapse was complete. In this run of playoff ineptitude, this may have topped them all. Perhaps, losing that final game of the year to the Phillies saved us from an even worse fate in the one-game playoff against the streaking Cardinals. Why is the thought "it could've been worse" so comforting? Unfortunately, there was soon to come a time when it really couldn't have gotten worse.

Chapter 14

Death, Taxes, and The Curse

The 2012 season was upon us. That eventful and appalling 2012. The Braves had flamed out in the playoffs in 2010. They had the historic September collapse in 2011. Is it even possible for 2012 to end in a more egregious way? Like has been said before – Death, Taxes, and The Curse.

The Braves were again right there at the end of the year. This time they actually held on to the wild card spot. However, as you might expect, the Curse showed itself again. In life, you understand there are circumstances that are simply coincidental, but the Curse takes it to a whole new level. Out of all the teams we could play in the one-game, winner-take-all Wild Card matchup, it was none other than those hated St. Louis Cardinals. However, Atlanta felt confident going into this single-elimination game. After all, the Braves had Kris Medlen pitching. Who's Kris Medlen, you ask? Well, Medlen became a starter midway through the year and proceeded to go 9-0 to end the season, with the Braves winning the final 23 consecutive games he started. TWENTY-THREE. Now, you tell me if you wouldn't have felt just as confident going into that game. Without a doubt. Stop me if all this sounds familiar. Braves make playoffs. Braves are favored. Braves…..I think you can probably fill in the rest.

Medlen chose this day of all days to have maybe his worst day of the year. Of course he did. Don't they always. However, all the blame can't be placed at Medlen's feet. In fact, by the end of this game not a single person will be talking about Medlen at all. The game started out well for Atlanta, as is the usual Curse protocol. They were up 2-0 into the fourth inning, with Medlen rolling merrily along. An innocent leadoff single in the top of the inning for the Cardinals was erased in a double play fielded by Chipper Jones. Wait, not a double play, you say? Not even close.

In this soon-to-be last game of the future Hall of Fame player's career, Jones picked this moment of all moments to have a Curse moment. The routine grounder was fielded cleanly, but as Jones attempted to start the double play, he threw the ball into right field. With slow-footed Matt Holliday running, it would have been the easiest double play of Jones' life. As you might expect, the Braves never get away with a play like that. What should have been an easy double play, leading to two quick outs, turned into a massive Cardinals rally scoring three runs. Isn't that how it always turns out. I can't say I can recall Chipper ever making such a poor throw to second base. In this game, however, when every play mattered, he did. And it was huge.

In the seventh, two more Braves errors led to two more Cardinals runs and a 6-2 deficit. Let's get this straight, the Braves, who were the BEST fielding team during the 2012 season, made three errors leading to a motherload of unearned runs in their absolute biggest game of the year. Sounds about right. In truth, Medlen did not pitch all that badly. His defense and his team let him down in every which way. This looked like another typical Braves postseason exit. However, the Curse wasn't looking for a typical ending this season.

The Braves came to bat in the bottom of the eighth, not knowing the fireworks were just beginning. The Braves put runners on first and third, with one out, and the tying run at the plate in Andrelton Simmons. The next play will long be remembered in Atlanta. Simmons hit a weak pop fly to left field. As he slammed the bat down in anger, thinking he may have just stifled the comeback rally, we all saw a miracle happen. The Cardinals botched the play and the ball dropped. It actually dropped. A moment of providence had finally swung our way. We were going crazy in my home. The bases were loaded, there was only one out and we had a chance, when all had seemed lost. My wife and I were leaping for joy. This time, though, I didn't lift her in exultation. Instead, I looked at her, forgetting for a brief moment where I lived, and said, "I can't believe it. Maybe our luck is finally turning."

Our luck was most definitely turning………for the worse. When all settled down, we noticed Braves Manager Fredi Gonzalez running onto the field arguing, pleading with the umpires. Apparently, umpire Sam Holbrook had called Simmons out on the infield fly rule. That is, if the ball is popped up on the infield with runners on base and an infielder is clearly perched under the ball, the batter is automatically out. This prevents the fielder from intentionally dropping the ball and getting the leading runners out. Sounds like a great rule for the offense, right? Well, perhaps it would have been, had the ball not actually been in LEFT FIELD. That's right, Holbrook called the infield fly rule on a play when the ball was halfway in the outfield. In the entirety of baseball history, I am confident there had never been an infield fly rule called on a ball that far into the outfield. Not only that, the Cardinals infielder was by no means settled under the ball. There was no rationale for making that call. Fredi Gonzalez was livid.

The Braves fans in the stadium were incensed. And, in my house, we were in a stupor of disbelief.

It was more than a terrible call. It was a game-changer. It was a season-ender. It had happened again. The Curse had risen and taken away our hopes. Kris Medlen was off the hook. Chipper Jones and the Braves' butterfingered fielders were off the hook. Even Andrelton Simmons was off the hook for popping the ball up. Now, it was all about the infield fly rule. It was all about the umpire stealing our season away. It was all about Atlanta and the Curse.

As if the play itself wasn't bad enough, the aftermath was worse. When the news began filtering through the stadium, anger filled the air like never before. Anger over the play and the call. Anger over all of the close calls throughout the years that had not gone our way. Anger over never being able to catch a break as fans. Anger over the Curse and all it had done to us. We were all angry and tired of this constant fiasco. The fans began throwing anything and everything onto the field – cups, bottles, batteries. I often wonder, who brings batteries to a baseball game? Did they come to the game with anarchy in mind? Were they arming themselves, like gang members before a turf war? Were they planning on buying some electronics on the way home? A flashlight, a walkie talkie, maybe a Tickle Me Elmo doll?

I hate to admit it, but if I had been there, I think I would have done the same (although, I probably wouldn't have had the requisite ammo). I was so incensed at what was transpiring. I am embarrassed to say I wanted the field trashed, not because I support such behavior, but because at that moment it all became too much to handle. I couldn't believe that call was made, in that situation, and neither could anyone else. The angst of an entire city had finally bubbled over and was spilling out onto the field.

That play, more or less, represented the end of the Braves rally. After the field was cleaned and play resumed, the Braves again went quietly into the night. Again, it was at the hands of the Cardinals. When games take on a title, such as "The Infield Fly Rule Game", you know they are impactful. Unfortunately, for our state, we have produced many such titles. Perhaps you remember some of them. "The Lonnie Smith Game", "The Jim Leyritz Game", "The Eric Gregg Game" and now this. Just say the name and everybody knows exactly what game you mean. In subsequent years, we will come to know games as "Second and 26", "10-0", and "28-3".

My least favorite part of losing games like these are the "day after" sports talk radio shows or social media vent sessions. I say least favorite, but they have become a necessary part of recovering from such disasters. And, unfortunately, they have become all too familiar. An entire sports town grieving over another lost season. Another season ending in anger, bitterness and disillusionment. These platforms afford the city and its fans an opportunity to vent, to lay blame wherever it may be placed, and to discuss our wretched, sinister Curse. Yes, the "day after" shows are cathartic, but they are played out. What about a "day after" victory show? Or a "day after" tweet-fest? How satisfying would that be?

The Fall of 2012 came and went. I hope to never experience a year like that again. I'd like another sports area to come up with four months more heart-wrenching than what my community witnessed. The Braves and the infield fly rule. The Georgia Bulldogs and their collapse against Bama in the SEC Championship Game. The Falcons and their collapse in the NFC title game. All of that in just four short months. FOUR MONTHS. Karma can never make up for what it has stripped from us. However, things will get so bad over the next seven years, 2012 will seem like a pleasant memory. I know that's hard to imagine, but it's true.

Believe it or not, the Braves returned to the Division Series again in 2013. This time against the Dodgers. Again the Braves were favored. Again they lost Game One. Again they lost the series. Ho-hum. Following that series, the Braves tore the team apart, realizing they weren't constructed to win it all. Truthfully, they probably were, but in Atlanta they really never stood a chance against the Curse. That four-year run was over, and the Braves went into playoff exile for the next few seasons.

In 2018, our Braves returned to prominence. A young group of upstarts, led by Ronald Acuna Jr. and Freddie Freeman, had surprisingly won their division. They headed to the playoffs as a decided underdog against the heavily favored and defending National League champion Dodgers. Maybe this time, we could pull the upset against a team that was supposed to win. Perhaps the noose would tighten around someone else's neck for a change. No, that didn't happen. The better team actually won this time. It's just that the better team, for a change, was not us. The Dodgers easily dismissed the Braves in four games. We can't win as favorites. We can't win as underdogs. Our streak of Game One losses had reached nine, and so had our postseason losing streak. Living through it all was one thing, but sitting back and reflecting upon what has happened renders it completely inconceivable.

The 2019 Braves, like all of the others before them, reeled us in again. We were near the top of the National League for most of the summer and cruised into the playoffs. The 2019 Braves were distinctly different that the previous year's edition. They now expected to win. We expected them to win. The youth was maturing, and it seemed like everything was falling into place. The playoffs began with a renewed hope, a rejuvenated sense of purpose. Our team was focused on breaking the Curse. And then Game One happened.

    I wish baseball would do away with Game Ones. If there was ever a case of needing to win a game for the sake an entire city's psyche, this was it. We had to win Game One. We had to put all of the previous failures behind us. We had to show our opponent that this team, this season, would be different. Oh, and did I forget to mention that our opponent was none other than the St. Louis Cardinals. Are you kidding me? Not these guys. Not again. To make matters worse, Sam Holbrook, he of the infield fly rule, was commissioned to work in this series. Of all the umpires they could have assigned to this series, don't you think Major League Baseball could have chosen another? Sam Holbrook? Really? Was this a conspiracy against my heart?

    Game One started like seemingly every other Game One. Atlanta took the lead early and held a 3-1 advantage into the eighth inning. The Braves bullpen had been a strength for the team ever since three midseason trades bolstered a beleaguered bunch. Everyone was clicking. Everyone except reliever Luke Jackson. Watching Luke Jackson was like sitting in the eye of a hurricane. It may seem calm for the moment, but you know the destruction is right around the corner. At least, we thought, he would not see action in this game or any other, unless there were unforeseen circumstances. This game was lining up perfectly for the Braves. Max Fried had shut the Cardinals down in the seventh in electric fashion. Fried had been a starter during the regular season, so he certainly could have kept pitching. My brother texted me after Fried obliterated the Cardinals in the seventh. We both agreed, there was no way you remove him from the game.

Alas, Braves manager Brian Snitker disagreed. He decided to do what all Braves managers have always done, he overmanaged. Teams that win the World Series generally hold to one truism, they win or die with their best players. During the regular season, the Braves best two pitchers were easily Fried and rookie Mike Soroka. Snitker, having weeks to align his pitching rotation for the playoffs, decided to use Fried out of the bullpen and only give Soroka one start in Game Three. If you're going to bring Fried out of the bullpen, at least let him pitch more than one blasted inning. Some managerial decisions have disaster written all over them. This was certainly one of them. Bobby Cox, er.. I mean Snitker, decided to sit Fried after the seventh and bring in Chris Martin. Martin was not a terrible option, he just wasn't Max Fried. Snitker was going through relievers like they were going out of style. Hopefully, Martin would have an uneventful inning.

It turns out Martin didn't give up a single hit. Unfortunately, he didn't even throw a single pitch. In the long history of the Curse we have seen a lot of strange things that have turned the fortunes of teams. Here was another. Apparently, Martin injured himself while WARMING UP. That's right, he got hurt tossing practice pitches. He was removed without throwing a single live pitch. Out came Snitker, who promptly brought in…..no don't say it……..Luke Jackson. If you had of been standing anywhere near the Braves stadium, I am convinced you could have heard an audible gasp from the crowd.

Luke Jackson had been a major source of consternation throughout the entire season for the entire fan base. How he even made the postseason roster is anyone's guess. Then on cue, boom…. bam…..boom as soon as he entered the game. In a flash, home run, single, single and Jackson was exiting the game after giving the Cardinals new life. Had Snitker left Fried in the game, there's no guarantee he would have shut down the Cardinals again, but I would have liked his chances. With momentum now in the Cardinals dugout, they took off, scoring six runs over two innings. Despite a Braves rally in the ninth, the Cardinals had given Atlanta another Game One loss, 8-7. This loss was like all of the others. And somehow, they always seem to be by the margin of a single run. This "game of inches" thing is a real killer. We were the better team and we gave the game away. It always happens. And it appears it always will.

    Who's to blame? Is it Snitker for pulling Max Fried out of the game for no legitimate reason? If you're telling me Snitker was saving him for the next game, that's hogwash. Every game is so crucial, you have to approach it like it's the last. That's what winning teams do. You don't save Fried for another day. You take what you can, when you can. Victories don't fall in your lap; you have to grab them. Is the blame on Chris Martin's faulty oblique muscle? That seems unreasonable, but it sure makes for an easy scapegoat. Do we blame Luke Jackson? Actually, he probably deserves the least blame. He can't help he's not a great pitcher. The results were predictable as soon as he was inserted into the game. Honestly, there is no one to blame but Tecumseh himself.

    The series wasn't over, though. The Braves dominated Game Two and had a miraculous comeback in the ninth inning of Game Three. You know what, we thought, maybe these Braves ARE different. In fact, in Game Four these Braves had the Cardinals down 4-3 in the eighth inning with two outs. We were so close to ending this abhorrent streak of series losses. Right about the time the Braves were setting up champagne bottles in their locker room, the Cardinals hit a broken-bat, bloop single to bring home Paul Goldschmidt, who had reached on a broken-bat, bloop double. The game was tied. Reliever Shane Greene had made all the right pitches, yet, as in every previous series, the sports gods smiled on our opponent. Bloop, bloop, tie game. Seems so easy. For them, yes. For us, never. As expected, at least by all of us forlorn Braves faithful, Atlanta lost the game in extra innings. Once it reached extras, we all knew it was over. It always is. However, everyone thought, we were still coming home for Game Five. The series isn't over, they said. We'll get 'em on our own field and do what it takes to win.

I feel sorry for anyone who really thought that. In my high school classroom, the Curse is well-documented. Before Game Five my students were asking me what I thought. As a seasoned Curse enthusiast, I told them to save their hope for something else in life. Not on these Braves. Not on any of our teams. They haven't experienced much of the pain. They're still in the innocent, naïve stage of the Curse. I warned them against investment. They should have listened.

Despite all of my Curse bravado, I was still nervously awaiting the game for two days. Finally, I sat down to turn on the game ten or so minutes after the first pitch. I wondered if Braves starter Mike Foltynewicz, who had pitched so brilliantly in Game Two, had shut St. Louis down in the first inning. As the screen turned on and the focus became clearer, I couldn't believe my eyes. I mean, I really couldn't. There had to be some mistake by the television network scoreboard at the corner of the screen. But there was no mistake. The score was 7-0 and Foltynewicz was long gone. Already? How? Impossible. And the inning was still going. When all was said and done the Cardinals had scored 10 runs. TEN. Let's repeat that. In the first inning, the Braves gave up a staggering TEN runs to the St. Louis Cardinals in the winner-take-all Game Five. At home.

Never have I seen the likes and never will I again. Every year, every season we say it can't get worse and yet it somehow does. We say we've seen it all, but invariably something unthinkable occurs. Could you imagine scoring tickets to this must-see event? How demoralized the ticketholders must have felt. Even worse, imagine if you arrived ten minutes late because of traffic, excitedly ran to your seat and looked up at the scoreboard. You know that had to have happened. Only the Curse can bring such misery. Of course, you can't recover from giving up ten runs in the first inning, and the Braves, accordingly, lost 13-1.

We certainly have had plenty of self-inflicted wounds over the years, but the Cardinals have done their fair share of slicing and dicing our emotions down to the bitter nub. They did it again in 2019. Can I please be the first to say, I never want to see a St. Louis Cardinal ever again? Ever. This was no doubt the most reprehensible moment in this inauspicious streak of series losses. Worse than Brooks Conrad and his three errors in 2010. Worse than the eighteen-inning travesty against the Astros in 2005. Even worse than the infamous infield fly rule game of 2012. There seems to be no way to stop the bleeding. Ever.

With the series loss to the Cardinals, the Braves, yet again, wasted a season. Let's count the records and marks of atrocity from the streak, including only the seasons from 2001-2019. Most consecutive Game One losses in playoff series history (10). Most consecutive playoff series lost in the history of baseball (10). Winner-take-all Game Five losses at home since 2001 (4). Series close-outs at our home stadium by the opponent since 2001 (8). And now, most runs allowed in the first inning of a postseason game (10). There seems to be no end in sight to the indignity. This is who we are and there's no reason to be ashamed. We are at the mercy of the Curse and there is nothing we can do to subvert its power. How much worse could it get, anyway?

Chapter 15

Dr J, Threezus And El Gigante

While the Braves were authoring front page Curse moments year after year for three decades, the Atlanta Hawks were barely newsworthy. In fact, in almost five decades of action, the Hawks had been in the NBA's version of no man's land. That is, the Hawks had landed smack-dab right in the middle of the pack almost every season. Good enough to make the playoffs, yet never great enough to really compete for the title. Their best chance came in those 1988 playoffs against the Celtics. Their only other real opportunity was thwarted by trading away Dominique Wilkins in 1994, which is the only time a league leader has moved its top scorer during the season. Now, that's true Atlanta sports. That equates to 48 seasons and absolutely nothing to show for it. Really, it's a shame, because I think Atlanta is an NBA town just waiting to break out. It just has never quite materialized. Truthfully, as with every other franchise in our city, the Hawks were probably only a couple of breaks away from realizing bigger things.

Case in point: the Julius Erving-led Hawks team of 1972. Wait a second, "Dr. J" played for the Hawks? Well, sort of. Erving, who was playing in the rival ABA league at the time, struck a deal to sign with the Hawks just before the 1972 NBA season. However, he was also drafted by the

Milwaukee Bucks, who believed he was their property. While the legalities were being sorted out, Erving joined all-stars "Pistol" Pete Maravich, Walt Bellamy and Lou Hudson for a couple of exhibition games with Atlanta. Word on the street was they were going to be unbeatable. In the end, though, the ABA worked the system, allowing Erving to remain in their league. Could we just spend a few moments here in pure speculation, dreaming of what it may have been like having Dr. J soaring through the Atlanta skyline? For a hot minute the Hawks were the sexiest team in the league. Instead of leading his teams to three ABA Finals and later to four NBA finals, he could have been transforming our franchise into a world champion. But, that didn't happen. Of course not.

In their first forty-eight seasons in Atlanta, the Hawks made the playoffs 31 times. And that's including an eight-year stretch with no appearances from 1999-2007. Thirty-one times the Hawks graced the postseason stage. Thirty-one times the Hawks failed to make even one conference final, among the last four standing in the league. We're not even talking about an NBA Finals appearance, just a measly semifinal round. Zero. Zilch. Nada. Just so you don't start thinking we're probably in good company, there were exactly three other teams to have accomplished that feat. The Charlotte Hornets, who had only been a franchise since 1988, had not made a conference finals. Neither had the New Orleans Pelicans, whose franchise only began operations in 2002. The third team is the Los Angeles Clippers franchise, which has been considered by most to be the absolute worst franchise in sports history. Yep, that's the company these Hawks were keeping, two expansion franchises and the bottomless pit of sports. For practical purposes, let's remove the relative newcomers Pelicans and Hornets from this discussion. That means there is a list of futility that includes only the Hawks and the CLIPPERS. That's like being on a list with New Coke. That's like saying the Hawks have been as successful as Chernobyl or the Hindenburg or the Titanic. Consider how much effort it must have taken to be that bad. But that's just it, they were hardly ever bad. They were worse than that, they were mediocre. They were average. They were the bachelorette that makes it past the first couple of rounds, but never makes it to the home-town dates. Not only have the Hawks never received the final rose and won the hearts of an entire city, they've never even been invited to the ceremony. Considering their putrid draft history, it's a minor miracle the Hawks have had as much success as they've had.

In 2014, everything changed. The Hawks were actually better than average. In fact, they were incredible. In just two short seasons, General Manager Danny Ferry had done the miraculous by shedding the terrible contracts of Joe Johnson and Marvin Williams, as well as letting over-priced free agent Josh Smith walk away. In turn, he was able to replace them with gritty, hardworking performers Paul Millsap, Demarre Carroll and Kyle Korver, to go along with our lone remaining all-star Al Horford. These Hawks were a team made up of no true superstars, but a starting five that worked perfectly in sync under Coach Mike Budenholzer's system. After a modest 7-6 start, they exploded, winning a staggering 33 out of their next 35 games. Consider, the record for most consecutive wins in the NBA was 33 games by the historic 1971-72 Lakers. Now, our bunch was keeping company with the other team from Los Angeles. This time, however, we were hanging with the big boys. The Lakers had been among the cream of the crop of the NBA elite for decades, and now (at last) my Hawks were too.

These Hawks were anything but flashy, yet they were sure fun to watch. My personal favorite was sharpshooter Kyle Korver. Perhaps, he was my favorite because he reminded me of myself (in my very best of dreams). He even had the greatest nickname I had heard in a long time, Threezus. In January, the Hawks became the first team in league history to go 17-0 in a single month. By months end, they had the best record in the entire NBA, including the fast-rising Golden State Warriors.

Over the last year, the landscape of the league had dramatically changed. Lebron James bolted the four-time Eastern Conference Champion Miami Heat for his hometown Cleveland Cavaliers. With the Heat dynasty broken up from within, the East was wide open, and the Hawks seemed primed and ready to move into the top dog position. Atlanta's rampage through the league in January led to an unusual achievement. For the first time in NBA history an entire starting five was named player of the month. Imagine that. They were one well-oiled machine and that acknowledgement told the story. In a year that just happened to see the Braves in last place, as well as severe regression from the Falcons and Bulldogs, the Hawks couldn't have come along at a better time. The stage was all theirs. To cap off the record-breaking first half, the Hawks had four players selected to the Eastern Conference All-Star Team, which was coached by Budenholzer.

Finally, Atlanta was an NBA town. Finally, we had a team we could be proud of. Finally, we had a team that had a legitimate shot at the NBA title. Of all the teams to defy the Curse, was it really going to be the Hawks? In league history, it is well-documented that championships usually require one major ingredient, a superstar. In fact, maybe two or three. Yes, our Hawks had four all-stars, but none of them would be considered among the very best in the league. The Hawks success was more of a result of "sum of their parts" and team chemistry. We had veterans that knew how to play with a common goal, and that took them to heights unimagined. I knew getting my heart invested in these guys was going to be a risky proposition, but could you blame me? The Falcons had let me down. The Dawgs had jilted us at the altar. The Braves had crushed my soul beyond all recognition. I had to give the Hawks at least a chance to rip my heart out and stomp it into the ground. And so I did. I was all in.

On February 6, the Hawks played host to the Golden State Warriors, in a matchup of the two best teams in the league. Neither team had really accomplished any playoff success yet, but this game seemed like an NBA Finals preview. Which team was going to take the vacated spot for supremacy? At that point, odds seemed pretty even. That night, my family just happened to be over at my brother's house and this game had all eyes glued to the television. What a game. The Hawks did what they did best and defeated the Warriors in front of a home crowd that seemed more hyped than ever. This was the statement win we had been looking for from the Hawks ever since those Game Six and Seven losses to the Celtics back in '88. Perhaps, we would be the team to rise and replace the Heat at the top of the league. Who cares if we didn't have a true superstar. We had a TEAM.

Every game had us enraptured from first tip to final buzzer. Even meaningless games towards season's end, when home court advantage was already secured were must-see. You didn't want to miss a moment. On March 30, versus the Milwaukee Bucks, we were rewarded. Some moments stay with you forever, good or bad. This one was ridiculously scintillating. On an average Monday night game, with the regular season winding down, in a game with nothing on the line, lightning struck. And by lightning, I mean Kyle Korver. In a tight game against the Bucks, in an instant, Korver went off. He hit four consecutive shots, scoring 11 unanswered points in one minute, in an amazing display of catch-and-shoot artistry. He was absolutely out-of-his-mind hot and the crowd knew it. After the first three makes had already gotten the packed home crowd in a frenzy, the Bucks missed a shot on their subsequent possession. The crowd rose to their feet as one, anticipating a chance to blow the roof off the arena. As the Hawks quickly came down the court, everyone, including the Bucks, knew where the ball was going – to Korver. On cue, Korver curled behind the ball-handler, received a pass well back of the three-point line and fired an off-balance heat check like no other. In that moment of magic, his fourth consecutive shot fell, and I saw visions of championship glory.

I know, Curse 101 tells you that heart-wrenching defeat is inevitable. Even still, I brushed my logic aside and jumped head first into Atlanta Hawks fandom. They coasted to the finish line and into the playoffs. I'll be honest, the Hawks really didn't do much to impress in the first two rounds, winning both series 4 games to 2. In fact, there were times in both of those series when I was sure the Curse was rearing its ugly head again, especially against the Wizards in Round 2. It seemed like every game saw Washington's Paul Pierce hitting another ice water-running-through-his-veins buzzer beater. But, somehow, in the end the Hawks prevailed.

Believe it not, after almost five decades of professional basketball in Atlanta, the Hawks were making a conference finals appearance, just one step away from the NBA Finals. We had finally done it. The opponent, Lebron James and his Cavaliers. This was our opportunity to knock LeBron off his perch and cement our place at the top. Even better than that, the Cavaliers were to be without two of their top three scorers for much of the series, Kyrie Irving and Kevin Love. Not that I didn't want to beat their team at full strength, but let's be honest.... I really didn't. More successful franchises have a right, if not a responsibility, to be bolder, but not us. We've got to "get while the gettin's good," as they say. This was our chance at NBA immortality. As a fan, I can tell you every Finals matchup over the past sixty years, including the runners-up. Just making it that far would be an amazing accomplishment. We would be remembered as more than just the franchise that drafted professional wrestling "legend" El Gigante. It was all right there at our fingertips. All that being said, we still had to beat the Cavs, and they still had the best player in the league.

Actually, this series would end up being a referendum on which design worked best, a team built around a superstar or a team constructed as "all for one, one for all". If we are being completely truthful with ourselves, we should have expected the inevitable outcome. Seriously. here we were, the Hawks and their best record in the East against the horribly crippled Cavaliers squad. Seemed like a walk in the park on the scenic route to the Finals. Surely, there was no way a team whose second best player was Matthew Dellavedova could compete with our "well-oiled machine". An entire year of evidence clearly showed we were the better team and this series would prove that.

We were so confident, my brothers and I even bought tickets to Game Two. Let me pause right here and let you know that dropping that kind of change on a sporting event is not my norm. In fact, it probably goes against everything I've done up until that point, but this seemed like a once-in-a-lifetime chance. I didn't want to miss out on something that could have been so monumental for Atlanta. I wanted to be a part of this Curse-defying moment and the circumstances were ripe for success.

But aren't they always? Did the Braves and their yearly march to the playoffs as the "best team", only to be exterminated by an inferior opponent, teach me nothing? If you listened very closely, you may have heard some clanging in the room next door, perhaps the dropping of "the other shoe"? Isn't that the way it always is and will always be? The fact that we were the higher seed and Cleveland's roster was so decimated, only served the Curse's purpose that much more. Did we not know the goal of our Curse by now? Build up our flights of fancy, then go all El Gigante on our city, body slamming our hopes and dreams. We made it too easy on the Curse, gave it too much leverage with our hearts. Lebron James was all the Curse needed and he showed up in spades.

For our part, we played about as poorly as we possibly could. Paul Millsap looked as if he'd aged ten years in a week, as Cavs forward Tristan Thompson flew around him like the road runner. Cleveland shooters JR Smith, James Jones and Iman Shumpert didn't have a Hawk within five feet of them all series. Records WERE broken. It's just we weren't the ones breaking them. Cleveland smashed all kinds of records for three-point shooting, which I guess means we broke records as well. Ours, however, were for futility and ineffectiveness. LeBron was great and we were terrible. That about sums it up.

My brothers and I went to Game Two, still with hopes of NBA Finals dancing in our heads. Unfortunately, it wasn't to be. All of the hype and anticipation, all of the excitement and unfettered joy that accompanies a game of this magnitude were stripped away almost immediately. The Cavs jumped on us early and never looked back. A 30-18 Cavs run in third quarter destroyed any faint hopes we may have had. We stayed the remainder of the game, but our arena, which once had seemed like a rock concert, now appeared as a morgue. And the Hawks were the corpses. The party atmosphere on Atlanta's MARTA transit system we witnessed prior to the game had been replaced by stunned, cold silence on our trip home. The game and series were effectively over. The Cavaliers swept the two games back in Cleveland and, in an instant, our magical season was finished. Once again, the long history of the NBA proved to be an accurate predictor. The team with the best player beat the team with the better, uh, team. Who needed chemistry when you had LeBron James? As we know, however, this wasn't at all about LeBron James. The Curse had won again. We were devastated again. My heart had taken yet another pounding. The Curse, however, true to its nature, was not finished with its business.

The Curse doesn't just bend our will, it is determined to break it. In June 2015, the Hawks parted ways with the team's architect Danny Ferry over racist comments he read aloud from a scouting report. The words, although ignorant and wildly offensive, were not his, yet he was held accountable for speaking them publicly. Losing Ferry was a tremendous blow to what the Hawks were building. Budenholzer stepped in to make all personnel decisions, but that ended up being an abject failure. Our city could now add to its "only in Atlanta" list. As in, only in Atlanta could the general manager, who almost single-handedly rebuilt our team from the scrap heap, ultimately lose his job over reading a racist scouting report. That's a perfect Curse moment and it was all ours.

The Hawks never returned to prominence. LeBron still dominated the East on his way to four more NBA Finals appearances. Worse than that, along the way, he led Cleveland on a journey to their own "curse-breaking" season in 2016. Isn't it great when your Curse helps other cities break theirs. Oh, and by the way, those upstart Golden State Warriors ended up being the team of the next five years, winning three titles with the "Splash Brothers", including that 2015 playoff season. They became the NBA darlings, while once again, we became the league's redheaded stepchild. By the way, did I tell you we once drafted El Gigante?

Chapter 16

The Grim Reaper Cometh

The Curse of Tecumseh is real. Its burden on our city and state is real. Every play, every decision, every call that favors the other team now seems like a Curse moment. To say we were gun-shy, is putting it lightly. However, even those of us who had been longtime believers in its stranglehold over Georgia sports, could not comprehend what the Curse had in store for us next. The Braves rainout of the 1982 baseball playoffs, some thirty-five years earlier, seemed like child's play by comparison. As did any other of your favorite Curse moments since then. We had gone through all types of trials and tribulations, seemingly hardened by it all, yet we would soon realize we were still wide-eyed, deer-in-headlight novices. The Fall of 2012 seemed calamitous, yet 2017 came and went like the Grim Reaper, leaving us lifeless and soulless, our bodies left as carcasses for the vultures.

As the college football season began in 2017, the Georgia Bulldogs had modest expectations. After our starting quarterback, Jacob Eason, got injured in the first half of the opening game, those expectations dropped precipitously. However, little did we know, inserting unknown freshman quarterback Jake Fromm may have been the most providential moment of the season. He got his feet wet in that first game against a vastly undermanned Appalachian State team, but that wouldn't be the case in the season's second game. The opponent for Fromm's first career start was none other than Notre Dame. At Notre Dame. At night. National television. Even the most optimistic of Georgia fans had to question our ability to escape South Bend, Indiana unscathed. This game, however, encapsulated who the 2017 Georgia Bulldogs would become. They were a senior-led team, who leaned on the best stable of running backs in the country, a stout and stingy defense, a young mistake-free gunslinger and a four-eyed kicker who became legend. On September 9, each of those elements was on display. When Rodrigo Blankenship kicked the game-winning field goal with 3:34 remaining, followed by a sack-turned-fumble from the UGA defense, the Dawgs season began in earnest.

Week after week yielded win after win. Senior running backs Nick Chubb and Sony Michel, along with freshman DeAndre Swift, were dominating each game on the ground. Jake Fromm was more than doing his part to keep the offense high octane. However, what made this team special was its defense, led by the tackling machine and missile of a linebacker Roquan Smith. UGA made it all the way to 9-0, flying up in the national rankings. Unfortunately, they did not make it to 10-0. A road trip to Auburn slapped the Dawgs back down to earth. Specifically, a 40-17 smackdown that left us reeling.

In previous iterations of the Curse, this would have been the death blow. Seasons past would have left us regretting the Auburn debacle, analyzing each "what if" sequence in the game (see Florida loss in 2002). The Curse, though, in its newest form, was not settling for such infantile setbacks. Losing to Auburn was a war wound for sure, but the Curse wanted to go in for the kill.

As fate would have it, Georgia had a second shot at Auburn in the SEC Championship Game, thanks in large part to the Tigers win against Alabama. Destiny sure seemed to be on our side. Although Auburn had thoroughly thrashed us less than a month earlier, anything was better than playing Alabama. We remembered all too well the collapse against them in 2012 and nobody was ready to relive that. That sentiment played out in the game, as Georgia annihilated the Tigers 28-7, winning the SEC title and sending Georgia to the College Football Playoff for the first time.

If I may be completely honest, almost immediately after the jubilation of winning the SEC title had subsided, my first reaction was not of excitement and anticipation, but one of dread. Dreading the aftermath of another big game Curse moment. I didn't know how or when it would occur, but I was confident Tecumseh had a juicy one waiting for us. Heartache had been doled out generously over the years, so why should this year be any different? At that point, we had been down this road way too often.

Truthfully, when the selection committee placed Alabama in the final four, it should have been clear how everything would play out. Think about it. Not only did Alabama not win their conference (that was Georgia, thank you), but they didn't even win their own division. That had "Curse moment waiting to happen" written all over it. It's not that you don't hope and root for the best. It's not that you don't want to feel the rush of championship glory. It's that, deep in the recesses of your heart, you know you never will. You come to expect the inevitable letdown. If you've continually been burned by relationships, you tend to never trust again. I am not ashamed to admit that I have trust issues….and rightfully so. They say it's better to have loved and lost, than to have never loved before. However, does that adage necessarily apply to sports? Is it better to have come close to winning and lose, than to have never been close at all? I guess the answer is yes, as I still keep coming back for more heartbreak season after season.

Little did any us know what awaited us in the college playoff, but it was insanity. The semifinal matchup against the Oklahoma Sooners in the Rose Bowl was significant, if for no other reason, than we were playing in the Rose Bowl. Once the game started, though, time and place stood still for anybody watching this game, one that became an instant classic. Oklahoma jumped out to a 31-14 lead in the first half, scoring on five of its first six possessions. We couldn't stop them. Sooner quarterback Baker Mayfield was doing his thing, swagging it up all over the field. At the end of the first half, Bulldog kicker "Hot Rod" Blankenship trotted out for what appeared to be a throw-away 55-yard field goal attempt. Incredibly, he made it. It seemed to be a galvanizing play for the Dawgs and sent UGA into the locker with the momentum having switched sidelines.

As the second half started, Georgia rode its running backs to 21 consecutive points and a 38-31 lead. With the lead toggling back and forth, Georgia tied the game with under a minute left to send both teams into overtime. Somehow, at last, it was OUR team that stormed back from a huge deficit. In the first overtime, both teams exchanged field goals. In the second overtime, Roquan Smith was everywhere, almost single-handedly willing this defense to rise up. On a crucial third down play, Smith came out of nowhere to stop a Sooner back in his tracks, on what looked like a certain first down run. The play, which should go down as one of the greatest tackles ever, sent Oklahoma to a fourth down field goal attempt, which Georgia blocked.

All we had to do was score and we win. And on second down, we did. Sony Michel raced 27 yards down the sideline into the endzone, setting off a celebration down South that I'm sure was reverberating in the Rose Bowl 3000 miles away. We had done it. In one of the most entertaining games anyone will ever watch, our team had come out on top. I must have re-watched the last hour of that game half a dozen times, feeling the same sense of exhilaration as when I saw it live. Winning the game in walk-off fashion was especially sweet.

Now, here we were. The Curse had been held at bay thus far and we actually had won the semifinal matchup. Could we finally put the finishing touches on a magical season or were we now going to blow it in the Championship Game? My heart was hopeful, but my Curse-sense was definitely causing much skepticism. We had defeated a formidable foe, but Goliath was lurking around the corner. That proverbial giant was, of course, Alabama. Isn't it always? I know the phrase says, "in order to be the best, you have to beat the best," but come on. Alabama had slid into the playoffs, having lost its final game of the regular season. But there they were, staring across at us on the battle field once again. Why couldn't somebody else have vanquished them for us? I thought Auburn had done just that, but the Curse writes his own scripts. Nothing would ever be easy. Even though we were the SEC Champions, it sure felt like we were the underdogs. If they were Goliath, I sure felt like David. Could Georgia somehow muster up five smooth stones and slingshot and actually slay the giant?

Visions of the 2012 game against Bama were still hauntingly vivid. A game that we had almost won, before our late game collapse. A game that should have been a precursor to a championship. A game that has been replayed over and over again in my mind. And here we were facing the giants once again. We knew it was going to be a steep hill to climb. In fact, it was quite the mountain. George Mallory, one of the first Mount Everest summit-chasing pioneers, was once asked why he pursued the mountaintop. His answer was so simple, yet so profound. He replied, "because it's there". Similarly, why do we hope to beat Alabama in this biggest of all games? Why do we strive against all odds to do something that might seem improbable? Why do we risk our emotions and put our hearts on the line? I defer to George Mallory to answer these questions.

Alabama was "there", but so were we. Perhaps, on paper it probably looked a little lopsided. They had a seasoned quarterback, who played for the championship the previous year. We had a freshman quarterback who was in high school the year before. They were the team that had won four championships since 2009. We were a team with none since 1980. Their coach, Nick Saban, was undefeated versus his former assistants. Our coach, Kirby Smart was one of his former assistants. I'll say this, though, after years of being favored in sporting events, being the underdog actually produced some unreasonable confidence.

Confidence? Did I seriously say that? Who was I kidding? This was Alabama. A-LA-BA-MA. Every sports outlet acted as if it was a foregone conclusion the Crimson Tide were going to win. As well they should have. Then they actually played the game.

As much as a team can dominate the first half, Georgia dominated Alabama. The halftime score of 13-0 didn't accurately convey how easily the Dawgs handled the Crimson Tide, stifling their offense and their quarterback Jalen Hurts. For the first time the entire season, I truly believed we could win the whole kit-and-caboodle. However, there is a big difference between "could win" and "would win". I'm sure Tecumseh was smiling, though, as our belief grew throughout the game.

When the two teams came out for the second half, Nick Saban had decided to bench his starting quarterback in favor of seldom-used, but highly-touted freshman Tua Tagovailoa. Who does that in a National Championship Game? You know who? Champions. Clearly, Saban saw that Hurts was not the quarterback that was winning this game. Tagovailoa may not have been either, but Saban knew he had to take a shot. Loyalty is a cute idea, but in reality, it has no place in sports. Bobby Cox could have had many more titles without such misplaced loyalty (see Charlie Leibrandt). Sometimes change for the sake of change is a terrible idea, but sometimes you hope to bring a player into the game with horseshoes in his pockets. Tagovailoa not only had horseshoes, he apparently had four-leaf clovers, rabbit's feet and any number of luck-inducing paraphernalia in his pockets.

We saw this on his first drive, one that actually ended in a punt. As we've seen time and again, there are plays that define games, and this was one. I'm sick and tired of these plays, that inevitably turn the fortunes of both teams. And they always turn our fortunes for the worse. No, it wasn't a big play from Alabama that changed momentum. It wasn't an ill-timed mistake on Georgia's part. It wasn't a great or poor coaching decision by either team. It was the worst type of game-changing play of all. It was a blown call by the official. Georgia blocked Alabama's punt attempt, which would have resulted in the Dawgs having the ball on the doorstep of the Tide endzone. A touchdown at that point most likely puts the game out of reach. For a brief moment my heart leapt, and I had the dastardly thought, "Oh my, we're about to win the National Championship."

For a brief moment we had Alabama by the throat, and backed in an inescapable corner. For a brief moment my thoughts were of confetti-filled victory parades and redemption. Then, the Curse said, "Not so fast!" The officials called an offside penalty on Georgia, negating the blocked punt. At first, we were disappointed, but then we saw the replay. Our player was distinctly NOT offside. The emotions turned from disappointment to disbelief. The disbelief turned to anger, as visions of umpires Eric Gregg and Sam Holbrook flashed before our eyes. Did anyone have any batteries? Why does every big, incorrect call go against our teams at the most inopportune times? The blocked punt was wiped away and the game moved along. Score one for the Curse.

This game was filled with play after play in which, had they gone Georgia's way, the game would have been effectively over. Case in point, was Alabama's next drive. The Tide were facing third down and seven, when Curse moment #2 occurred. Tagovailoa rolled right and backwards, seemingly losing yardage with every stride. UGA defenders were all over Tua, about to sack him for a huge loss, setting up a crucial punt. As if he was covered in Vaseline, he somehow slithered away, racing across the field for a nine-yard gain. If that same play had occurred one hundred times, Tagovailoa would have been sacked ninety-nine of them. There was no way he could escape, and yet he did. Of course he did.

Sensing new life, Bama marched down the field for a touchdown, getting right back into the game. One fingernail shy of bringing Tua to the ground. One split second of action turned a devastating loss of yardage into a life-saving first down dash. Plays like the missed sack change history. Destinies are changed. Identities are formed and reformed. That could have been the play that turned our football team into a champion. Or a dynasty. We'll never know. Tua turned a horrible mistake into a beautiful gallop. The Curse had 2, the Cursed had 0.

This Georgia team was not going to just roll over, though. They immediately came back for a long touchdown strike to receiver Mecole Hardman. Then, we picked off Tagovailoa and had the ball in Alabama territory midway through third quarter up 13 points. Certainly, this was familiar to the Georgia faithful. We were at a very similar juncture back in 2012. Could we please just lay the hammer down this time? Score here and the championship will be a foregone conclusion. Cut the head off the snake. That thought lasted all of eight seconds, as Jake Fromm was intercepted on the very next play. The very next play! How many chances were we going to get? Surely, Alabama felt like we had given them life, where there was none (again). Can someone just make THE play that will release the vice grip of the Curse on our sports teams? Curse moment #3 was in the books.

The teams exchanged punts for the next few possessions, until Bama drove down to the Georgia 7-yard line with under four minutes to play. The Tide had fourth down and were still down by seven. Can we make just one more play? The mantra "just make one more play" has become a familiar phrase around these games over the years. It doesn't seem like that big of an ask, but it sure has been pretty difficult to come by. If we stop them on fourth down, we can bleed the clock down to almost nothing. One play, please. As my brothers and our families watched this game, we all stood up, yelling at the screen for just one more play. I'm sure we weren't the only ones. Tua rolled left and threw up a fourth down prayer. He couldn't take a sack, so he just tossed the pass into endzone, hoping for the best.

I remember, once as a kid, my brother Tim and I were playing a dice game. He challenged me to toss one of the die to the other end of the table and into a bottle cap. I could have tossed that die for years and never have made that shot. However, in that rare moment sitting at my kitchen table, I unflinchingly made the shot of a lifetime. The die had bounced twice before gently nestling into the bottle cap. Needless to say, we both went bonkers. I threw it, hoping for the best, with no real expectation of actually making it. I can assume Tagovailoa felt much the same as he sent his prayer of a pass into the endzone. He threw it and hoped.

Prayer answered. Receiver Calvin Ridley, cutting across the back of the endzone, just happened to be in the right place at the right time. Tagovailoa couldn't have possibly seen him, none of us could, but somehow the ball found him. Somehow, Alabama's last chance landed in the arms of their own. Did we really expect anything less? Still, the small, quiet voice in my head was questioning if it was even real. I couldn't believe my eyes, but I really shouldn't have been surprised. Those sort of plays had actually become the norm. A fourth down, blindly-thrown heave into the middle of nowhere turned gold for Bama. Georgia had to suck up yet another deflating, game-altering, legacy-creating play. Curse 4 - Dawgs 0.

We clearly knew at this point that the Curse would not let us win. Every time we were a single play away from riding off into the sunset, we were abruptly awakened from our premature daydream. And, just as we thought, Georgia gave the ball right back to Alabama, who drove straight down the field. The Tide ran the clock all the way down and lined up for a short 36-yard championship-winning field goal. I looked at my wife and told her to grab the kids. My brothers were standing beside me in stunned silence, as we had blown another golden opportunity. As we were preparing to collect our hearts off the floor, something happened. Something so unlike anything our sports town has seen. Something that can only be described as Curse-breaking. Alabama MISSED the kick.

In that moment, I witnessed the most authentic display of pure joy I had ever seen. It was akin to surviving a plane crash. Certain death was imminent, yet, unbelievably, we were alive. Overtime was upon us, just like against Oklahoma. Are you kidding me? This type of drama in back-to-back games? Perhaps we could have a second walk-off victory, this time for all the marbles. What I should have realized, though, was that every prolonged second of the game, only served to make a loss that much more painful. But, you know what? I didn't care. Alabama hadn't won…. yet. Our souls hadn't been crushed…. yet. The Curse had actually given us one back…. Yeah right!

In overtime, Georgia actually lost nine yards and had to settle for a 51-yard field goal attempt. However, as we saw against the Sooners, Rodrigo Blankenship had nerves of steel and a titanium toe. He split the uprights, again sending my brother's living room into delirium. We were up by three. One stop and we're dancing. One stop and Goliath would be slain. One stop and the Curse would be no more. A slip, a fumble, an interception, a penalty. Anything to end this state-wide misery. It was all right there.

On Bama's first play, Tua did what he did all night, he scrambled. This time, however, the freshman backup quarterback was not covered in Vaseline or any other petroleum-based substance. This time, he was not able to slither away. This time, the Dawgs sacked him for a 16-yard loss. At last, we had gotten the play we needed. We felt like Ralphie from the *Christmas Story*, desiring only his much-coveted Red Rider BB Gun, in spite of his mother's "you'll shoot your eye out" protests. And much like Ralphie, we threw caution to the wind. All of our dreams were very likely just moments away. The one thing we wanted more than anything else was gift-wrapped right in front of us. How could we possibly "shoot our eye out" now? Delirium turned into pandemonium. Ecstasy. Frenzy. Free-for-all. You name it, we felt it. Second down and twenty-six yards to go. I repeat, TWENTY-SIX yards for a first down. TWENTY-SIX yards from our long-awaited National Championship. TWENTY-SIX yards away from redemption. This was it. If Alabama's kicker couldn't connect from 36 yards, he surely had no shot from 58 yards out. We were about to win it all.

And there it is. This is what the Curse had been waiting for. He had given more than ever. Gave us an SEC Championship. Gave us a Rose Bowl overtime victory. Gave us a big lead in the Championship Game. Gave us a lead in overtime. Gave us a second-down-and-TWENTY-SIX-yards-to-go away from the title. Gave it all to us, except one thing. The Championship itself. Cue Tua Tagovailoa. Cue "shooting our eye out". Cue the Curse.

They say there are moments when time stands still and life flashes before your eyes. One second can change a lot. One second, in this case, changed the fates of all constituents. The players. The coaches. The fans. The legacies. It all was rewritten in one split second. Tua dropped back and let go a 41-yard pass to a streaking Crimson Tide receiver. Not a single Bulldog in sight. Touchdown. Game over. Overtime walk-off victory.... for Alabama. In an instant, we went from victory to agony. From immortality to oblivion. Redemption was gone. We literally went from celebratory hugs to silence and devastation in a second. How is that even possible? Was it really over just like that? From the highest of highs to the lowest of lows faster than you can say Tecumseh. Even for us, this had reached a new level tragedy.

There was no recovering from this collapse. The sticks of dynamite had been strategically placed around our hearts and the ensuing implosion was complete. While the many years of Curse-dom had taken a toll, this went well-beyond anything we had previously witnessed. My subsequent sports stupor was not a pretty sight. Unlike the Rose Bowl, I couldn't bring myself to relive this game for quite some time. Could you blame me? At least, as a sports community, we had finally reached rock bottom. There was only one place to go, up. Right?

Chapter 17

The Backup Plan

Self-reflection is a difficult process. Many times, even when the truth is staring us right back in the face, we see only what we want to see. A couple of truths, however, smacked me right upside the head after the latest Alabama loss. UGA and Bama were not rivals. In my mind, a rivalry is a two-way street. A rivalry means both teams have had signature wins in the series of head-to-head matches. The last time the Dawgs won a game against the Tide was back in 2007. Since then, we have been their whipping boy, so to speak. Every game has been significant and every game we have come up short. The disappointing part is, despite the final outcome, we have generally been the better team.

Secondly, I realized that we were not David going up against Goliath. David actually never lost to the giant who stood before him. Not only are we not David in this scenario, we are among the many nameless foes that Goliath pummeled into rubble. Yes, we were the underdogs. Yes, we were up against the most feared and powerful opponent in the land. Yes, we fought fearlessly to the very last. However, in the end, we were not the ones standing over their fallen opponent in victory. Our battles against Alabama remind me of the movie *Independence Day*. In the film, aliens (the bad guys) come to earth in an attempt to exterminate all mankind. The earthlings (the good guys) try everything they can humanly think of to defeat the invaders. In one particular climactic scene, the humans strike the space ships with the biggest weapon in their arsenal, a nuclear bomb. However, in spite of the fact it was the best they had, it was still rendered ineffective. In much the same way, UGA had thrown all they had at Alabama, only to continuously come up short. Let it be noted, at movie's end, the aliens were soundly and permanently defeated. Now, I'm not suggesting we infect the "mothership" Alabama with a virus to achieve victory, but there has to be something that hasn't been thought of yet that would yield ultimate success.

    Revenge and redemption are two concepts that are intrinsically linked, yet so vastly different. As a fan of UGA, the question became which of the two was our fan base after? Revenge is born out of the darkness of circumstance. Revenge is fueled by motives that generally smack of desperation. Revenge is not driven by internal purity, but rather by achieving success at another's expense. Redemption, however, is more of a heroic endeavor. Redemption is looking inward, through times of struggle and adversity, in an attempt to bring out the best from deep within. Redemption is all about virtue, integrity, and strength of character. I'd like to think our goal is an incorruptible shot at long-sought redemption. We want our best to finally be THE best, regardless of who the opponent may be.

    However, truth be told, I think we want to stick it to those pretentiously smug Bama fans as much as anything else. We know they view us as lap dogs, but for once, we'd like to be the masters of our domain. In either case, there was only one way to achieve both. We needed another opportunity at Alabama, and the 2018 season would be a crusade to make it a reality.

There was no doubt UGA fans took an emotional beating in 2017. Not only did our team come away empty again, they came as close to a championship as any team in the history of college football had come without winning. It was more than brutal. In a game we thoroughly dominated, the only time we were behind was the final play of the game. If that's not Curse-worthy I don't know what is. Imagine losing a game of that magnitude, where if any one play goes a different way, we win. How do you recover from such heartache? Well, if you're Georgia, you hop right back up on that pony. Go out and do it again. And so they did.

As has been said before, the most agonizing part of our Curse is a very difficult thing to pinpoint. Is it that we have simply won fewer titles than every other sports city? That's certainly up there, but futility alone does not make a curse. Is it that we have had so many opportunities for titles, deep playoff runs, or teams set up perfectly to win, only to have fate deal us a fatal blow in the end? Yes, those missed chances will never be forgotten. Had things played out differently in just a fraction of those situations, this would all be a moot point.

However, to me, the absolute worst aspect of this scourge is the manner in which these wasted opportunities have played out. For one, every loss has been preceded by that moment of belief. A moment, perhaps ever so brief, when you just know you're about to be crowned champion. It is also the myriad of different ways in which our teams have gone down, many of them leaving you shaking your head in confoundment. It is the bewildering coincidences, the unfortunate broken records and the sickening turn of events that seem to always accompany the losses. We don't just lose the big games, we do it in style. We exit with a storyline that has never been written before, and likely will never be written again.

The 2018 Georgia Bulldogs would be no different. UGA was once again among the top teams in the country, controlling most games with relative ease, earning an 11-1 record, and earning another shot in the SEC title game. We were, after all, the reigning SEC Champions. This time, though, we weren't playing Auburn, the team we brushed off without a sweat the year before. Nor was it a team that would give the Bulldogs or their fans any reason for displays of bravado.

It was the old nemesis, Alabama. Again. We couldn't get rid of these guys. They were like the archetypical villain that keeps coming back from the dead. They were the neighborhood bully that will only relent once punched in the mouth. We just hadn't punched hard enough yet. They had become accustomed to stealing our lunch money, pushing us off the swing set, and giving us a fat lip after school for just looking at them. Were we actually ready to stand up to them once and for all, not wilting at their slightest threats? Were we finally prepared to take on the role of Rocky and go toe-to-toe with Apollo Creed, Clubber Lang, Ivan Drago or any other of his highly-favored opponents? For the second time in just eleven short months we had to face our familiar, tormenting adversary. Like a bad penny, they kept turning up. All we asked for is a reprieve, if for only a year. Regrettably, it was not to be.

On December 1, 2018, Georgia faced Alabama, once again with everything on the line. As the game got underway, the tone was eerily reminiscent of the previous matchups. Let's see if this sounds at all familiar. Georgia got off fast and strong. Again, they appeared to be the far superior team. The Crimson Tide seemed nervous, tight, and quite frankly, overmatched. Bama was dropping passes left and right, missing assignments on critical plays, turning the ball over, and generally being outplayed by Georgia.

Tua Tagovailoa, now the starting quarterback for the Tide, was getting swarmed by the Dawg defense all game. He hardly looked like the player who had been at the top of the Heisman race for most of the year. In fact, his performance in this game was reminiscent of Jalen Hurts' performance against Georgia the previous season.

Prior to the game, I can't say I was even cautiously optimistic. Same road, same destination. However, every Georgia score and every Tide miscue drew me in a little more. By midway through the third quarter the Curse had me again. I want to formally express how much respect I have for Tecumseh and his Curse. I keep telling myself not to fall for its ploys, and every year I so easily get suckered in. Celebrated showman P.T. Barnum once famously said there's a sucker born every minute. Oh, how would he have loved me. I get swindled and hoodwinked in such lamentable ways every single time. And it happened again.

Talk about regrettable moments. With 6:20 remaining in the third quarter, another Georgia drive had stalled. Rodrigo Blankenship came out to kick a short 30-yard field goal. Keep in mind, Blankenship was one of the best kickers in the country. He had only missed three kicks all year, and one of those had been blocked. Certainly, he hadn't missed anything as short as this.

Knowing all of that, I spoke the words that I wished I could have brought back almost immediately after I said them. I yelled to my wife, Misty, who was in the other room, "If we make this kick, we're gonna win this game!" She was in the other room for several reasons, none coincidentally. First, she didn't have the nerve to watch. Secondly, she wanted to shake things up a little from what she had done the last few big games. However, her primary reason for not sitting with me, was to prevent me from doing the premature "wife lift". I concurred, believing it's better to be safe than sorry. Instead, I did the premature guarantee. As soon as I uttered those dreaded words, I felt the pit in my stomach. I heard the cackling of the Curse in the background. Oh yeah, and I heard my wife yell back, "Why would you even say that, haven't you learned your lesson?"

But let's all be completely honest with ourselves. If your team was up 14 points midway through the third quarter, with your All-American-caliber kicker lining up for a 30-yard field goal, you'd have been confident too. Also, consider that had he made the kick, Georgia would have been up by 17 points, with little more than a quarter remaining. That's a THREE-SCORE lead. I had every right to be bold. Which is precisely what the Curse wants and lives for. Somehow, despite watching the 2012 SEC Championship Game, the 2018 National Championship Game, and almost every other big sports moment in my life, I still had belief in what my eyes were telling me. And once again, I was fleeced.

As you may have already guessed, Blankenship missed the easy field goal, giving Alabama hope where there was about to be very little. I yelled out a horrifying scream at the shanked kick, only to hear my wife say, "You shouldn't have said anything. You knew that was going to happen." I realized, right then and there, the Curse's authenticity had finally been recognized my wife. She had now been around the block of sports disasters a time or two herself and was well aware of Curse etiquette. As soon as Blankenship missed the kick, I felt it all come flooding back. All of the angst. All of the memories of our grim history in big games. My thoughts immediately switched to curiosity. Wondering, in what dastardly manner was the Curse going to do us in this time?

After Alabama scored to make it 28-21 going into the fourth, we were all in full Curse-watch mode. With just over twelve minutes left in the game Alabama began a drive that would change the fortunes of both teams in ways nobody could have imagined. Early in the drive Tagovailoa, who had been crushed several times throughout, had to exit the game due to an injury. In came Jalen Hurts. I'm sure you remember him. Jalen Hurts, the starting quarterback for the Tide in last year's championship match. Jalen Hurts, the one who was replaced by Tagovailoa midway through that game. Jalen Hurts, the guy who saw his backup lead his team to an improbable comeback victory. Now, HE was replacing Tua? I promptly texted my brothers, already envisioning what the Curse would have in store for us. Last year's game was a torture-filled experience. We regularly said that was the worst way to lose. Well, Tecumseh had different designs. What could possibly be worse than losing a championship where the backup quarterback leads the opponent to a miraculous comeback? THIS. As famed New York Yankee Yogi Berra once said, "It's like déjà vu all over again."

Watching Tagovailoa replace Hurts and win the game for Alabama last year was terrible. The thought of Hurts now replacing Tagovailoa and returning the favor was almost too incredible to have even imagined. Georgia came into this game hoping for redemption, but it was Hurts who might actually get it. The circumstances behind what we were witnessing were downright impossible. On the drive which Hurts came in, he made one big third conversion after another. We couldn't get him off the field, as his fresh legs were evident. It seemed like we had him in third and long every play. And every play he converted. After a 16 play, 80-yard drive that churned up over seven minutes of clock, Bama had tied the game behind Hurts.

Georgia's next drive showed their desperation after blowing ANOTHER big lead. Their drive having stalled, they lined up to punt on fourth down. With so little time remaining in the game the prudent thing would have been to punt Bama into a corner, deep in their own territory. Playing for overtime, where momentum matters a little less, would not have been the worst decision for a Dawgs team that was reeling. However, Coach Kirby Smart decided to fake a punt and go for the first down. Let's just say the play failed miserably, giving Alabama the ball around midfield. It was a horrific call at the most inopportune time. Some might argue that had it worked, we'd all be praising coach Smart. But it didn't, did it? It never does and it likely never will.

After Alabama and Hurts completed another third and long pass, they quickly scored to take the lead with 1:04 left in the game. Just like that, Georgia winning went from a foregone conclusion to a pipedream. With a minute left, Georgia drove down the field, giving themselves one last play just 39 yards away. The last-gasp pass fell incomplete. Did any of us really think we had any magic left in us? Was there ever any magic to begin with anyway? If there was, it was all on the other sideline. And just like every other year, that moment of finality had come. We had been defeated.

The loss was bad enough, but the circumstances surrounding the loss were excruciating to live through. Losing to Alabama's backup in back-to-back years. Losing a game in which you dominated for much of it for the second straight year. Losing another game where all you had to do was make just one more play. The Curse was not jabbing us with gentle body blows any more. It was an all-out barrage. It sensed weakness, smelling blood in the water, and went in for the kill. We were like chum, tossed out in the ocean, just waiting for the inevitable circling of sharks.

Consider the following piece of information, as well. Georgia had lost to Alabama for the second consecutive year. The total time the Crimson Tide had led the two games was 1:04 COMBINED. We had lost two of the biggest games in our school's history, eleven months apart, while only trailing ONE MINUTE and FOUR SECONDS. Incredible.

Georgia had come into both games as the underdog. Yet, in both games they more than outplayed Alabama, controlling the game from the onset. In both instances, the Tide quarterback who started the game was not the one who finished it. In fact, the players and their roles were completely reversed. In both games, Georgia seemed to have every intangible factor in their favor, including revenge and redemption. In spite of that, Alabama came out ahead when it mattered most, when the clock read 0:00. There was no revenge for the Dawgs and the only redemption was for Hurts. They say these types of games are unpredictable, but that is generally lip service. However, absolutely nobody could have predicted this turn of events. The funny thing is this was not even close to the most undeniably heinous Curse moment in our dubious sports history. NOT EVEN CLOSE. Cue Tecumseh. Cue rock bottom. Cue 28-3.

Chapter 18

28-3...Need I Say More?

If it seems as though we've been building up to some pinnacle of failure, some collapse so epically historic, some Curse moment that tops all others, well, you're right. Let's not pretend this game is unheard of in any sector of the known universe. In every curse there has to be some moment that is generally agreed upon as the lowest of all. For the Curse of Bambino, it was Bill Buckner of the Boston Red Sox letting the ball trickle between his legs, allowing the New York Mets to win Game Six of the 1986 World Series. For the Curse of the Billy Goat, it was the Cubs blowing Game Six of the National League Championship Series, when a fan named Bartman infamously robbed a catch from Cubs left fielder Moises Alou. For us, there are many games that would have been considered the signature Curse moment for any other city. But those couldn't even come close to our top moment, our crowning achievement. There is one moment so abhorrent, so inconceivable, that it stands head and shoulders above the rest. We are speaking of none other than Super Bowl LI.

My father taught me much throughout my life. Most lessons I took to heart and still carry with me to this day. Lessons on driving, athletic endeavors, education, finances, marriage and fatherhood will always remain a part of me.

Time and again, my father's advice has been proven sage and valid. To me, his words were gold and needed no additional affirmation. If he said it, I believed it. Accordingly, I took his advice in all areas of my life. All areas, except one. From the time my brothers and I could walk and talk, he warned us to never trust our local sports teams. He cautioned us that teams from Georgia will "always let you down". As boys, we dismissed this out of sheer youthful defiance. As we matured, we rationalized our father's words as merely an effort to poke fun at our diehard allegiance. Now, some forty years of empirical evidence has led me to this very distressful conclusion. He was right. There can be no doubt about it. And as if we needed any more proof, February 5, 2017 was undoubtedly it.

The Atlanta Falcons had the type of season I had been dreaming of. For years, our town has provided us sports teams that excel throughout the season, only to lose to the "hot" team in the playoffs. This time, however, we were that hot team. After a modest 7-5 record through the first three quarters of the season, the Falcons went into supernova mode. They rampaged through their final four regular season games, averaging 38.5 points per game. It was unreal and they seemed unstoppable. Finally, we were the team that was peaking at the right time. We even caught a few breaks along the way and landed a number two seed in the playoffs, earning a first round bye. If ever there was a team built around a high-flying, high-octane, try-and-outscore-us-if-you-can offense, this was it. Quarterback Matt Ryan put up MVP-winning numbers, Julio Jones was Julio Jones, and all other pieces fell into place. We played fast and were blowing past every other team with relative ease.

In the divisional playoff round Atlanta blitzed through the Seattle Seahawks 36-20. In the NFC

Championship Game, the Falcons demolished the Green Bay Packers 44-21. And before we could blink, our suddenly torrid Atlanta Falcons were Super Bowl bound. At 7-5, it appeared we were headed for another mediocre season. However, we caught lightning in a bottle and streaked right into a championship matchup against the NFL's standard, the New England Patriots. That's right. Tom Brady. Bill Belichick. Spygate. Deflategate. Gronk. Dynasty. All of it and more.

Before Super Bowl Sunday, it seemed as though every commentator was picking the Patriots to win. Had they seen these Falcons at all? They had crushed every opponent mercilessly for six straight weeks. I knew the Patriots were going to be favored, but was everybody really discounting my Falcons? Had they seen their offense or their speed? Even among the fans, sixty percent of bets were placed on the Patriots. I understood. These were the PATRIOTS and we were the falcons. The team with a championship ring for each finger, against a team that hadn't even been window shopping for jewelry yet. The city well-versed in championship parades against the city well-versed in day-after vent sessions. Yet, albeit foolishly, I believed.

For some reason, this felt different. I think all Atlanta sports fans would agree, this Falcons team seemed distinctly anti-Curse. Perhaps, it was due to their unexpected run taking all of us by surprise. We didn't really have a chance to think about it. It's like going to see a good movie you've heard nothing about. You have no expectations. You bring no preconceived notions to the table. Often, those are my favorite movies, supporting the idea of ignorance is bliss. I can't say for sure if Falcons fans were ignorant as to what was taking place, but we were absolutely blissful. The town hadn't been this alive since the 1991 Braves.

Perhaps, this team felt different in part because of the curse-breaking that seemed to be all the rage. Baseball had seen the Red Sox, White Sox, and Cubs all break their own curses within the last decade or so. Basketball had seen the Cavaliers break Cleveland's long-suspected curse in a dramatic NBA Finals against the Golden State Warriors. By all accounts, this seemed like the very best chance to break ours, especially considering the horrors we had faced only a month earlier in the College Football National Championship Game. After Georgia's brutal loss to Alabama, the consensus was it couldn't get worse. We believed this unexpected Falcons' march to the Super Bowl was the redemption we'd been starving for. It had to be, if only because the thought of losing again with everything on the line was shuddering. The year 2016 could go down in history as the Year of the Broken Curse, if only we could seal the deal. This had to be the time our wretched Curse of Tecumseh finally ceded.

Our sports teams had come oh-so-close to championships over the past five years. The Braves, Bulldogs, Hawks, and Falcons all had opportunities that, for most teams, would have resulted in titles. Yes, fourth quarter collapses had become all too familiar, but at some point you'd think we'd get at least some of the crucial breaks to go our way. The Cubs had their moment in 2016. The Cavaliers had their moment in 2016, as well. Both teams broke their long-standing curses in historically dramatic fashion. Both teams improbably overcame 3-1 series deficits, which emphatically announced their breakthrough victories. Everybody in Atlanta felt like this was our moment. Our breakthrough. Our announcement. Just release the horses and let them run.

And did they ever. When Super Bowl LI started, the Falcons were off like a prized thoroughbred at the Kentucky Derby. They looked like the much faster team.

They looked like the much fresher and younger team. In truth, they looked like the much better team. Atlanta shot out of the starting gate like lightning and was losing sight of their challenger. The Patriots couldn't seem to catch their breath. When Robert Alford intercepted Tom Brady and returned it for a touchdown, the score was 21-0 and this game was all but over. At least in our minds. We had seen our city blow lead after lead over the years, but as I've said, this appeared otherwise. The Falcons had thrashed six consecutive opponents, and this looked no different. Matt Ryan looked every bit the MVP, while Tom Brady looked washed up. Our defense had all the answers, while the Patriots hadn't slowed us down yet. This was a runaway of epic proportions.

    We didn't get that lead by trick plays or lucky breaks or playing above our heads. Instead, we were playing exactly as we had the last six games, fast and loose. In those six games the Falcons had amassed an incredible 234 points. What we were witnessing was just the next domino to fall on our way to one of the most dominant championship runs in history. Nobody would forget these Atlanta Falcons.

    One thing concerned me, though, during our commanding first half performance. The Patriots held the ball for the last 8:48 of the first half. Several times drives were sustained on the backs of third down penalties by the Falcons. Though it only led to three points, I had some slight concerns about how much the Falcons' defense would have left in the tank. This was a story line that had followed these Falcons. In many of their wins Atlanta had jumped on their opponents early, only to see the defense tire in the end. In each of those other games, however, the lead was so insurmountable it didn't matter how many garbage points we gave up. So, honestly, I wasn't overly worried. As the second half wore on, nothing looked different. The Falcons were clearly the better team, eventually scoring again to take a 28-3 lead. Can we spend a moment to discuss this juncture in the sports universe? At 28-3 my father, the one who said you can never trust teams from Georgia, stood up and said to his three sons, "I'm going home and getting in bed. It looks like you boys will finally get one.". Even he was convinced the Falcons had this one in the bag. At 28-3, even my wife was secure enough to let me lift her up in celebration. I believe I said something like, "Finally, I can do this without fear of retribution."

I admit it, I am the dumbest human being to ever walk the face of the planet. But seriously, it was 28-3, for goodness sakes. It was a 25-point lead. Even a lead of 24 points would have resulted in more caution, as that would have "only" been 3 touchdowns and 3 two-point conversions away from tie. But 25 points? That meant New England would have to score at least four times to win. Keep in mind, we were already midway through the third quarter. Even if the Falcons didn't score again it would be virtually impossible to lose. But even at that, the Falcons offense showed no signs of slowing down either. This game was over. The fat lady wasn't singing just yet, but she was past her warmups and had made her way to center stage.

In 1999, the Falcons were improbably in this EXACT situation against the Denver Broncos during Super Bowl XXXIII. Only the roles were reversed. Atlanta was down by twenty-five points in the second half, just as these Patriots. I remember the feeling of emptiness watching that game. We knew it was over. Even when the Falcons returned a kick for a touchdown to cut the lead to eighteen, we knew it didn't matter. No one in the room back in 1999 was talking about comebacks. Every point we scored from then on would be for pure cosmetic purposes. At 28-3, the Falcons had a win probability of 99.8%. Can you imagine?

That probability implies that only 2 out of every 1000 situations like this would find the Patriots actually winning. The data supported that as well. Since 2001, there had been exactly ZERO wins by the trailing team under these circumstances in 190 opportunities. In fact, there had been only four such comeback wins in NFL history, including regular season. Forgive me, if I liked those odds of bringing home the Lombardi Trophy. Forgive me, if I lost all sense of Curse decorum and unfortunately performed the "wife lift". I'm telling you, at this point, the wife lift has become quite the source of contention in my home. It's almost become part and parcel of every single big game collapse. Perhaps I've become obstinate about the whole thing and I'll continue to stubbornly and ritualistically lift my wife in exultation until we finally see it through to the end.

    As my brothers and I sat there reveling in our championship aura of elation, the game almost became an afterthought, giving way to joy and frivolity. But if we were all being honest, we knew we could never get totally comfortable. Amid all of the hootin' and hollerin' there was always an underlying nervous tension among us. Still, it was TWENTY-FIVE points? We even tried to give lip service to the Curse, saying things like, "All it'll take is one play to turn this whole game around" or "We've been down this road before." But it was hard to pay Tecumseh the legitimate homage he deserved when the game was as lopsided as it was. We had actually (and ridiculously) started throwing out words like "Falcons dynasty". Talk about putting the cart before the horse. I bet, though, had we walked into any Falcons viewing party, we'd have heard the same dialogue.

    Had my Curse radar been on full alert, recalling the Falcons' twenty-five point deficit in 1999 would have genuinely given me the heebie-jeebies. I know the way our Curse works. It loves these uncanny coincidences. In fact, some may say it actually creates them out of pure diabolical villainy. I, for one, say it was less coincidence, than it was typical Tecumseh. Consider our past failures, and the devilish pattern becomes quite obvious. Charlie Leibrandt on the mound in Game Six thrillers in consecutive World Series was our first experience with such quirks. Seeing Leibrandt blow it in 1991 was bad, but the second time left us completely confounded. UGA losing to Alabama's backup quarterback in consecutive seasons with the National Championship on the line was utter ridiculousness. It was the only thing that could have made the second loss worse than the first. These sneaky twists of fate are precisely what drives the knife of sorrow deeper. Being on the positive side of a twenty-five point lead in this Super Bowl was the perfect Curse twist. What's worse than trailing by twenty-five and losing a Super Bowl? What about leading by twenty-five and losing a Super Bowl?

The Curse also relishes breaking records en route to our emotional decimation. The Braves have set the standard for futility by losing a record ten consecutive postseason series. Since winning the World Series in 1995, the Braves have had more dramatic losses and heartache than most cities have endured in their entire sports history. Jim Leyritz, Eric Gregg, and the Infield Fly Rule, among many others, are supreme lowlights, yet they all get trumped by the record streak of failure. The Bulldogs have broken records in both the SEC Championship Game and the College Football Championship Game for biggest leads lost. Each successive blown lead is more heinously disheartening than the previous. Even the Falcons themselves, hold the record for largest NFC Championship blown lead. But 25 points? Come on.

More than anything, though, the Curse loves bringing us to the height of jubilation on the biggest stages, only to pull the rug from beneath us. In the 1991 World

Series, Terry Pendleton's gap double had us jumping in exultation from what we thought was a championship clinching hit. That was promptly followed by the stark realization that Lonnie Smith had not scored, but was instead decoyed at second base. In 2018, the Dawgs sacked Alabama quarterback Tua Tagovailoa for a sixteen-yard loss in overtime that had an entire state celebrating a soon-to-be title. Unfortunately, one second and a 41-yard bomb later, Alabama was dancing in the streets. These are just a couple of examples in a long line of moments that ripped joy away in an instant.

    By the time the Falcons had built their twenty-five point lead, we were well-educated in such Curse bliss-busters and seemed to be growing more resilient by the year. Not that we were necessarily proud of our ever-thickening skin. At no time in our sports history, however, had we been this high. WE were humiliating the PATRIOTS in the SUPER BOWL by a score of 28-3. It most definitely could not have gotten better than that. And that's exactly what the Curse wanted. The higher the belief, the deeper the eventual despair.

    The avalanche started gradually, as New England scored a touchdown on a drive that was a fourth down completion away from ending the game. At fourth and 3 from midfield, had the Patriots failed to convert, they almost certainly would have been resigned to losing. Beyond that, they would be giving the ball to Atlanta in prime scoring position. Alas, the Patriots converted and proceeded to score. Even that, though, came with a missed extra point. We knew we weren't going to shut them out, but six points this late was harmless. So they converted one fourth-down play. New England was desperate and that should have played into our hands. They were already resorting to out-of-character trick plays and gambles.

Certainly, one of those would fail and end their misery for good. Or so we thought.

The theme of "just make one more play" would be threaded throughout the remainder of the game. After the touchdown, the Patriots went for an onside kick to get the ball back, but the Falcons recovered. This, like so many other plays, should have effectively ended things. But it didn't. The Falcons even started their drive with a nine-yard pass to New England's 32-yard line. If we had just done two quarterback sneaks and kicked a field goal the game would have been out of reach. Unfortunately, the Falcons were flagged for a ten yard holding penalty, pushing them out of field goal range and forcing a punt. All we needed was one play and the game was over. Just one play.

On their next possession, New England drove the field and settled for a field goal themselves. At this point, with under ten minutes remaining in the Super Bowl, the Falcons were still up sixteen points. That is two touchdowns, to go along with two 2-point conversions. To anyone with any football knowledge, a comeback at this point would have seemed like an impossibility. However, at our viewing party, the uneasiness started to mount. My brothers and I almost immediately ran those numbers in our head and thought aloud how typical this would be for Atlanta to blow this game of all games in this fashion. Two touchdowns with a two-point conversion, leading to an overtime loss. That sounded about right. The numbers just lined up too perfectly not to be ultimately meaningful. I'm sure that was a conversation that happened in many places around town. We had just seen this too many times not to notice the early Curse rumblings. Some might say our unbelief was a root cause in the ultimate demise, somehow sending a cosmic message into the ethersphere allowing the collapse to take place. But could anyone really blame us for our cynicism?

It was really on the next Falcons drive, though, where things began to unravel. The Falcons faced third and 1, needing to run the clock out or force the Patriots to use their timeouts. The obvious play call here is a simple run. The Patriots hadn't necessarily stopped us all night on offense. There was no need to get fancy, if you're the Falcons. Run the ball, get the likely first down and the game would be over, for all intents and purposes, with three additional plays to run time off the clock. Just make one more play. One.

Instead of the obvious hand off, offensive coordinator Mike Shanahan dialed up a pass play that changed everything. As Matt Ryan dropped back to pass, running back Devonta Freeman missed a crucial block (shocker), allowing the Patriots to sack Ryan, causing a fumble and flipping momentum in a heartbeat. What should have been a game-sealing run play turned into a game-turning fumble. As could have been predicted, the Patriots scored quickly, then successfully converted a 2-point conversion, incredibly cutting the lead to eight points. The only people more ecstatic than Patriot fans were the television commentators who finally had a game on their hands.

For our part, we were now in full panic mode, recognizing this for what it was – the greatest of all Curse moments. The Falcons had just gift wrapped a touchdown to New England. Had the Falcons run the ball on third down, even unsuccessfully, the Patriots would still have had little chance. Running the ball would have either burned 40 seconds off the clock or forced a precious Patriot timeout. Beyond that, the Falcons also could have punted the Patriots deep in their own territory, forcing another long drive when time would not allow for it. However, that never happened. We had our opportunity for the "one play" we needed, and we didn't take it. Go figure.

For all of the plays that could have ended the game prior to this, the next Falcons drive provided the coup de grace. Freeman caught a pass from Ryan, racing thirty-nine yards. A couple of plays later, receiver Julio Jones made THE play. In what can only be described as a Super Bowl-clinching catch, Jones made what would have gone down as one of the most clutch and magnificent receptions ever. His acrobatic, sideline tiptoeing, circus catch of 27 yards put the Falcons at the Patriots 22-yard line. Literally, we celebrated as if we HAD won the Super Bowl. Jones had made the "one play" we had been looking for. At this point, New England's chances looked bleak, to say the least. We knew it. The announcers knew it. The Patriots knew it. Everyone knew it except the Falcons play-caller Mike Shanahan. At this point, the only way we didn't win is if we did something stupid.

One of the most awe-inspiring things to watch is the implosion of a large building or structure. In the blink of an eye, what was once a monument of greatness becomes a pile of rubble. What once looked as if it could stand the test of time, is demolished into a soon-to-be forgotten ocean of waste right before your very eyes. That night, I saw an implosion like no other, a complete destruction of what once had looked invulnerable. Even horror film junkies would have had to look the other way for fear of "losing their lunch". Here we were, once again, at the precipice of victory. Triumph, celebration and parades all seemed imminent, if not a foregone conclusion. Yet it became another moment of "this is finally our time", ingloriously followed by the should-have-been-anticipated "What just happened?" As you know by now, highest of highs followed by lowest of lows. Getting old?

It is well-documented that teams with a lead do better to "go with what got you there" when trying to close out a game. I generally agree with that mindset. Our team was unquestionably built on an unfettered offensive scheme and a "letting it fly" attitude. In fact, that's exactly what we did on Freeman's 39-yard catch and Jones' 27-yard masterpiece earlier in the drive. It had worked perfectly. But there we were at the Patriots 22-yard line. Time for aggression was over. The Patriots were toast had we simply taken three consecutive kneel downs. The clock would have run down and the Falcons would have kicked a game-icing field goal. Unfortunately, Shanahan didn't see eye to eye with every other human being on planet earth. After a first down run (good call), Shanahan called another passing play (terrible call). Ryan dropped back and was sacked. Again. The twelve-yard loss was bad enough, turning a short field goal into a longer one, but let's don't compound things by doing anything else foolish. If we just run the ball, we can maybe gain a couple of yards, creating a more-than-manageable field goal attempt. At least, that's what we thought should have happened. Well....it didn't.

On third down, Shanahan called yet another pass play. This time the Falcons were flagged for another holding penalty, moving them back ten more yards and out of field goal range and a replay of third down. After ANOTHER pass play (are you kidding me?) fell incomplete we ended up punting the ball back to New England with three and a half minutes remaining. Self-inflicted wounds are one thing, but this was a full-on self-assault. This was jumping into a lake with a cinder block tied around your ankles. It was like running into a burning building with a can of gasoline. It was like walking out on a tightrope with no safety net......and no tightrope. What were we doing to ourselves? Didn't we want to win? All we needed was just one play, at any point in time, and it never came.

Only an hour earlier, when the score was 28-3 and the city of Atlanta was preparing for a celebration like no other, at this point seemed like a distant memory. The sight of us joyously prancing around the television high-fiving and chest-bumping was long gone. My father had probably been sound asleep for two hours, excited to wake up and talk championship with us. Midway through the third quarter New England had only a two-in-a-thousand chance of winning. That's like Doctor Strange telling Iron Man in the Avengers saga there was only 1 out of 14 million possible outcomes that had the superheroes defeating the villainous Thanos.

Wait a second. Are we actually playing the part of Thanos in this analogy? Even worse, are the Patriots the Avengers? Regrettably so. And much like Thanos, it seemed as if our catastrophic collapse was "inevitable". Ironically, it is a quote by Thanos himself that described how we all felt.

"I know what it's like to lose..... It's frightening. Turns the legs to jelly. I ask you, to what end? Dread it. Run from it. Destiny arrives all the same. And now, it's here."

Yep, that pretty much says it all. Destiny was knocking at our door, but none of us really wanted to answer it. It was here, nonetheless. Had we provided destiny a chauffeur and rolled out the red carpet to accommodate its arrival? No doubt. The time for Tecumseh to make his appearance was nigh, and we all felt it.

After punting the ball back to the Patriots, they drove down the field again in their typically surgical way. All the breaks were breaking for them now. We knew which direction the winds of fate were blowing when a tipped ball turned into a miraculous ground-scraping catch by Patriot receiver Julian Edelman. There is no way that ball gets caught in any traditional universe. Even watching the replay still leaves me befuddled as to how he ended up catching it. Did I really see what I just saw? I know things hadn't gone our way over the last quarter or so, but this play? Are you joking? I challenge anybody to watch that play unfold and come up with any fathomable conclusion other than the FACT that our city is cursed. Edelman's catch encapsulated the entire comeback. There was no doubt now the Patriots would score and eventually win the game. The writing was on the wall and Edelman's catch put the exclamation point at the very end of it.

Those long Patriot drives in the first half were now taking their toll. Our defense was gassed. Still, through it all, we simply needed just one play. One interception. One fumble. One dropped pass. One slip. Anything. We waited prayerfully, yet absolutely nothing came. Boom, boom, boom right down the field for another touchdown. After all of that, with just 57 seconds remaining, if we could just prevent one tiny 2-point conversion we would be Super Bowl Champions. The success rate of a conversion is less than fifty percent. New England had already been successful once, but certainly not twice? If we had simply made one stop, at that moment, all would be forgiven. Nobody would remember the collapse. Nobody would remember the boneheaded plays. Just one stop, right now, and we win. One play.

It wasn't to be. The Patriots succeeded again. Tom Brady was Tom Brady. And the Falcons were done. Overtime was about to ensue and that has been historically bad for our town. Let's briefly recap. For the Braves, extra innings have been a veritable postseason nightmare. Game Seven against the Twins in the 1991 World Series was lost in extra innings. The deciding Game Six against the Blue Jays in the 1992 World Series was lost in extra innings. The pivotal Jim Leyritz home run game against the Yankees in the 1996 World Series lost in extra innings. The record-breaking 18-inning loss to the Astros in the 2005 clincher also comes to mind. And there were many, many more. The Dawgs had lost to Alabama in overtime just one month earlier. Truthfully, we were still reeling a little from that disaster. So, when this overtime came upon us we had no expectations of anything good happening. We knew better. Had there ever been a coin flip that was ever less in doubt than this one? We all knew New England would win the flip. In fact, if you looked close enough, you may have even noticed Tecumseh in a striped shirt tossing the coin. It was fated, just like always. Of course the Patriots won the coin toss. Did anyone actually expect anything different?

  Brady opened up with five consecutive completions against the walking dead Falcons defense. All we needed was a special play from someone. Anyone. At this point, however, not a single one of us expected it. Our jaws were still agape at what had transpired. Shock was setting in. As was the anger from the forthcoming inevitable loss. A couple of plays later New England was in the endzone, celebrating under the confetti, having just completing the greatest comeback in Super Bowl history. But there are two sides to every coin. As the Patriots were putting on championship t-shirts, Atlanta was walking off the field after suffering the largest collapse in Super Bowl history. While Tom Brady was hugging Giselle and lifting his children amidst a throng of praise and glory, the Falcons were sitting shell-shocked in front of their lockers answering questions about their historic choke job.

The obliteration was complete. You can't recover from something like that. Not our team, nor our city. The Falcons should have just blown the team up then and there. It was pointless trying to trot the same group back out there the next year. The scars of this game were permanent and too damaging to build anything meaningful back up again. The same went for the city. This avalanche came with complete destruction, and it will take a long time to heal from these wounds. If ever. Within the span of one month, our town had experienced UGA's crushing collapse in overtime against Alabama and the Falcons devastating collapse against New England. Is this reality? Have I been asleep in some bizarre dreamland where everything turns out to be a nightmare? How has this possibly happened? Again, the symmetry is uncanny and typical of our Curse. Both teams had large leads, both suffered large collapses. Both teams needed only one play at any point to win, yet never finding one. Both teams losing to the crème de la crème of their respective leagues, the Patriots and the Crimson Tide. It was a disaster of biblical proportions. The walls of Jericho had fallen, and we were at the very bottom of the resulting mass of destruction. Midway through the third quarter of both games we thought our teams would never be forgotten. We were right. Their collapses will forever live in infamy, and the numbers "28-3" and "2nd and 26" will be etched in time.

 My father ended up having the final word on this turn of events the day after the Super Bowl. After reflecting upon what had happened, he turned to us and said these words that have become immortalized in our family:

"They almost had me this time… You just can't trust teams from Georgia, they'll always let you down."

Chapter 19

Sisyphus

If history (and movies) has taught me anything, it's that the good guys always win in the end. Can we please ruminate on this thought for a moment? Did Tecumseh have it right this entire time? Are we deserving of total destruction, dying in a dramatic combustion of flames? Or, do we represent the phoenix rising from the ashes of a scorched earth? In my mind, we were always the good guys. However, now upon reflection, could it be that we are actually the villains? Were we Thanos? Were we Ivan Drago? If not, then how else do we justify always finding ourselves under the foot of the heroic victor at the end of each movie? These are questions that are swirling around in my mind, with no answers to be found. Perhaps, we are the protagonists. Perhaps, the antagonist. Perhaps neither.

Maybe we are Sisyphus of Greek mythology. As the legend goes, after being punished in death by the gods for his self-adulating ways, Sisyphus was forced to roll a giant boulder up a mountain for eternity. Every time he would near the peak, the boulder would roll back down. He was condemned to endure perpetual failure. He was condemned to getting close without ultimate success. Does that sound like any particular forlorn city you may be familiar with? Perpetual failure. Tantalizingly close to achieving the ultimate goal. For eternity. Even at that, there are still questions. Are we Sisyphus the hero, never giving up in the face of an insurmountable task, demonstrating virtue through perseverance? Are we Sisyphus the punished, having to endure the same bitter fate for the remainder of time, never attaining the goal? Maybe we should call our plague the Curse of Sisyphus? Maybe not.

Forty years of reflection has taught me plenty. Sometimes only in hindsight can we see what was right before our eyes the entire time. Only now is it possible to see the ever-so-planned progression of the Curse. Participating in big game after big game, only to lose time and again in such tormenting fashion. However, for the Curse of Tecumseh, that wasn't good enough. It wanted to bury us. It wanted us to cry "Uncle!" It wanted to strip every shred of sports dignity away from us. It wanted to destroy every vestige of our sports humanity. Simply losing wasn't good enough. We had to lose in the most absurd, record-breaking ways, so implausible, we still have trouble wrapping our brains around the impossibilities.

And that is precisely what the Curse has done. Imagine, within a span of one month, we lost a College Football National Championship and a Super Bowl in games where we trailed for exactly ZERO seconds. I repeat, unbelievably, we trailed in neither game until the very last play. Incredible. To lose like that once is tough enough for a city, but twice? In a month? We know uncanny coincidence rides shotgun beside the Curse, but this was just unreal. I challenge any city or fan base to produce a more mind-blowing, punch-in-the-gut set of circumstances. In fact, that just may be the most incredible and outlandish of all Curse moments. Perhaps, the perfect capper to all of our "only in Atlanta" moments.

We have been dealt knockout punch after knockout punch in recent years. Yet, has there ever been a city that has shown greater fortitude and resolve? We keep getting knocked down, yet we somehow continue to come back for more (Sisyphus the hero?). Admittedly, it gets harder and harder every time. Why do we still care, when the final result is no longer in doubt? Our teams WILL get close and our teams WILL find a way to lose. It's sad to say, but at some point I lost belief in obtaining the prize (Sisyphus the punished?).

Hope and belief are certainly not the same. Yes, I always have hope in my heart, but my mind tells me it is misplaced. Truthfully, I'm jealous of fans that still have belief during those moments of consequence, even if it is misguided. It must be nice. It must be fun. For those of us who have been invested in Georgia sports teams for any significant time, there is nothing fun about what we have gone through. In fact, watching demise after demise has sucked much of the joy out of our attempted championship runs. No longer do we imagine ways we could win, but rather we envision only what may go horribly wrong. And so far, it almost always has. My wife, like many others, was not a Curse convert at first. She couldn't understand how one play in a game would turn my countenance so abruptly sour, especially in games we were leading at the time. Now, though, she is a true believer, as she has seen those seemingly insignificant plays become permanent momentum changers much too often.

To always be just one play away is a difficult position to be in. If Lonnie Smith doesn't forget how to run the bases, the Braves win the 1991 World Series. If the referees don't blow a call on a blocked punt, UGA wins the National Championship in 2018. If Kyle Shanahan simply has Matt Ryan take a knee, instead of passing late against the Patriots, the Falcons win Super Bowl LI. Those are just three of countless "one play away" moments that we have been forced to endure. Can you really attribute all of those to pure luck? Or even worse, can you really say it was all due to chance occurrence? I contend there is little evidence for the case of "pure chance". Let's investigate.

For argument sake, let's remove any Curse moments outside of semifinal or championship matchups. That means removing regular-season failures, late-season collapses, first round playoff upsets, or any other general sports oddities. Let's analyze the last thirty-nine seasons for each my Braves, Falcons, Hawks and Dawgs. That is, let's examine only the seasons of my remembrance, specifically only those seasons in which my teams controlled their own destiny and were two steps or fewer away from the title.

With those parameters in place, there were eighteen such instances. Let's repeat that, so there is no misunderstanding. My teams have been either one or two steps from a championship EIGHTEEN times during the years of my sports-conscious memory. And that doesn't count the 1981 UGA football season, when the Dawgs went into their bowl game with hopes of a championship, given a Clemson loss. Nor does it include the 2018 Dawgs, who were minutes away from beating Alabama for the SEC Championship and securing a birth in the College Football Playoff. Among all of the postseason appearances we have witnessed since 1980 (59, to be exact), eighteen times we had as good a shot as any to bring home the title. Eighteen shots at ultimate triumph, many of which we were favored to win. Many in which we had large leads and experienced a subsequent collapse. Eighteen times we have been among the final four teams, including nine occasions in the championship game. With all of those opportunities staring us right in the face, my teams have come up with exactly ONE title. I don't want to hear the naysayers suggesting we should be grateful for the one. Are you kidding me?

Let's spend a few moments doing a little math. We have come home with the crown once out of eighteen times. That is 5.6%. Repeat, we have been successful 5.6% of the time when reaching at least the semifinal round. Considering a semifinal consists of four teams, chance alone dictates we would win 25% of the time with such a reasonably large sample size. I know I'm a statistics teacher by trade and numbers come naturally to me, but that's pretty glaring, right? In statistics, there is a principle called The Law of Large Numbers. This law states that as samples increase in size, the closer the probability of success trends to the true value, according to random chance. However, statistically-proven laws can be summarily dismissed when referencing Georgia sports teams. Probability Theory can't stand up to the weight of the Curse.

Let's investigate further. We have been in nine championship rounds, coming away with just the one title. That is an 11.1% success rate. Perhaps you can help me with my math on this one. If you are among the final two teams, doesn't that equate to a 50% win probability, all things being equal? Let's say that again. By chance alone, we should have won 50% of those titles, yet we came away with only 11.1%. Keep in mind, in many of these matchups, WE were the favored team. When looking at either the semifinal or the championship rounds, the numbers say we should have won FIVE TIMES more championships simply due to chance outcome. Those numbers are absolutely mind-boggling.

If you wanted to extend things a little further, consider the teams I support (Hawks, Braves, Falcons, and Bulldogs) have appeared in 44 postseason rounds in which they were one of the final eight left standing. One title out of 44 opportunities is a 2.3% success rate. Random chance dictates a one in eight chance should result in a 12.5% success rate. Yet again, the numbers suggest that we should have approximately five times more championships purely by chance. Those numbers don't lie. If you think that it's a bit of stretch extending things to the quarterfinal round, consider the following. Over the last 23 baseball seasons the World Series has been won by the Wild Card team seven times (including three times by teams that finished behind the Braves in their own division). That is, the last team to sneak into the playoffs has come away with the title 30.4% of the time. Think about it, Wild Card teams have to play a single elimination game just to make the final eight teams. And, as we've seen, even those teams have routinely beaten the odds. In other words, although playoff outcomes really may be a dice roll, our numbers still never seem to come up.

To put things in a little more perspective, the Florida Marlins have made the playoffs exactly twice in their brief existence, which began in 1993. This was roughly around the same time the Braves began their playoff streak. Both years the Marlins entered the playoffs as the Wild Card team, finishing behind the Braves. Both years the Marlins won the World Series. Over roughly that same time span beginning in 1991, the Braves have made the playoffs 19 times (usually as the prohibitive favorite to win it all) and have come away with only the one championship. The Marlins, one of the worst franchises in sports, have two World Series titles. The Braves, the model franchise to many, have only one. Don't tell me about "odds" or "probabilities". Seriously, you really have to think long and hard as to which franchise you would rather support. That alone, should exemplify the state of things around here.

I refuse to accept the rationalization by others that say, "it was just chance" for why we have so few titles. That's complete hogwash. Bologna. Malarkey. You don't have to cook the numbers to see that "snake bitten" doesn't even begin to describe our status. Random chance says my teams should have won at least five championships. Tecumseh says we only get ONE and, thus far, his voice has spoken the loudest.

Could you imagine, though, how different our city's sports persona would be had we won in just half of our opportunities? We'd be right up there with some of the best sports towns, which probably would have resulted in even more titles. Winning breeds winning. We would have been a destination city for superstars. Everything would have changed. No, our teams aren't the Celtics or the Yankees or the Patriots or the Crimson Tide, but they could have been, had things fallen the right way. Has there been a town that has had so many wasted opportunities? There is unequivocal regret for what could have been, but apparently it was just never meant to be. And if it was meant to be, something has done a tremendous job of preventing it.

There can be little doubt that we have encountered some unspoken obstacle when approaching the finish line. It's as if our sports teams have been trying to breach some hallowed barrier over the last four decades, and Gandalf from *The Lord of the Rings* is standing between us crying out, "You shall not pass!" Much like our heroes from Middle Earth, we are also in search of a ring. Ours, however, is of the championship variety and we crave more than just one. And instead of Gandalf, we are held at bay by Tecumseh, unrelentingly and unyieldingly so.

For anyone that hears our story, they will agree that our Curse is a real, tangible phenomenon. It doesn't matter what we call it, Tecumseh or not, it is a legitimate inhibitor to our success. The weight that is felt by all of our teams in the critical moments is real. It is difficult to erase or escape our past failures. Why do you think Kirby Smart went for the ill-fated fake punt at the end of the 2018 SEC Championship Game? He was desperately attempting to exorcise the demons of previous losses to Alabama. He felt the weight of the twisted and despicable Curse. Why do you think the Braves choke in every elimination game? They feel the weight of the Curse and it's sabotaging every futile attempt to rise up and make a play. Will anyone ever make a difference-making play again? Who knows. The Falcons had dozens of opportunities against the Patriots, yet all attempts were rendered ineffective. Do you think they felt the weight of the Curse? Without a doubt. In the fourth quarter of the Super Bowl it was the Falcons who looked like the team hanging on for dear life.

    As has been said, sports is a game of inches. From what I've seen, I can vouch for that. Our town has seen games turn on a needlepoint, such narrow margins between winning and losing. The ledger can be tipped in either direction with such indiscriminately small actions. How is it, then, destiny always seems to nudge things just far enough the other way? I'm not sure frustration can adequately describe the emotions of a city that has seen such cruel fate. We have been defeated in every conceivable way. Unfortunately for us, our debates are not centered around which is the greatest team in our history, but rather which team has suffered the cruelest of fates. Curse-ology has taught us there will always be a new and unimagined way to lose. Oddly enough, however, these experiential lessons have led to an interesting character development within our fan base.

    We have built up quite an immunity to the venom of the Curse. What else can it do to us? Will the Braves lose 11 or 12 or 13 straight postseason series? Big Deal. Will the Bulldogs lose yet another title at the hands of Alabama after leading the entire game? Who cares. Will the Hawks march through another season of mediocrity? Great. Will the Falcons lose a Super Bowl in which they led by 26 points? So what. Nothing can faze us anymore. We have become bulletproof, or as the song says, "I am titanium." It's a freedom that has been hard-earned, and it puts us in rarefied air. I now revel in the fact that our city's Olympic mascot "Whatizit" has been universally considered the worst in history. I'd rather have it no other way.

We have formed a certain solidarity in our failures. We are bound by our historic collapses. And together we continue to pursue what has been unattainable. My perspective is not one of a professional athlete or a sportswriter or television commentator. I represent the fan, the "every man" of sports. Without us there are no dynasties. Without us there are no storylines. Without us there is no ESPN, because nobody would care. What we feel matters. Our experiences matter. It is OUR thrill of victory and agony of defeat that matters. In reality, the athletes and the sportswriters and the commentators are the spectators, watching and waiting for our reactions and our opinions. Those are the only measurables that truly matter in sports.

If there is a Curse, it is because we believe there is one. And you know what? I believe. The Curse of Tecumseh is real, not because it has a name. It is real because we say so. Perhaps, though, calling it out and giving it a name will take away its power; and this seemingly eternal stretch of residing in a championship abyss will finally come to an end. That is my dream, my hope.

Regardless, like the phoenix, we will come back every season for every one of our teams, in spite of the smoldering ashes. We will continue to live for those moments at the end of games, those moments at the end of seasons, that define who we are. Like Sisyphus, we will never stop pushing our boulder up the indomitable mountain. Whether we win or lose, I will be there lifting my wife in the air with utter jubilation. And one of these days it will be because the Curse has been lifted. One of these days Tecumseh will give up, but I never will…

NOT-*lanta*

Georgia. Sports. *Cursed*?

Jeff Lalaian

Visit www.notlantabook.com